Cold Feet

the best bits...

Cold Feet

the best bits...

Compiled by

Geoff Tibballs

GRANADA

Acknowledgements

The author would like to thank the following for their help and co-operation in the making of this book: Andy Harries, Christine Langan, Mike Bullen, James Nesbitt, Helen Baxendale, John Thomson, Fay Ripley, Robert Bathurst, Hermione Norris, Jacey Salles, Declan Lowney, Mark Mylod, Nigel Cole, Tom Hooper, Tom Vaughan, Pete Travis, Ian Johnson, Fiona McCormick, Susanna Wadeson, Nicky Paris at André Deutsch and the crew of *Cold Feet*.

Cold Feet is a Granada Television Production

First published in 2000
by Granada Media
an imprint of André Deutsch Ltd
In association with Granada Media Group
76 Dean Street
London
W1V 5HA

www.vci.co.uk

Copyright © Granada Media Group 2000

Geoff Tibballs is the author of this work and has asserted his right under the Copyright, Designs and Patents Act 1988 to be identified as the author of this work.

A catalogue record for this book is available from the British Library

ISBN 0 233 99924 8

Jacket design by Leslie Barbazette
Page design by Design 23

Printed and bound in Great Britain by Butler & Tanner Ltd

1 3 5 7 9 10 8 6 4 2

Contents

Introduction by Mike Bullen
Creator of *Cold Feet*

If I'd known, when I pitched the original idea for *Cold Feet* to producer Christine Langan over a lunch in Soho, that four years later we'd be shooting our third series, I'd have let her pick up the bill. This, of course, is said in jest. Christine paid anyway – no writer willingly reaches for their wallet when there's a TV exec. at the same table. The point I'm trying to make though, is that neither of us expected my at-that-time less-than-fully realized idea (a typical writer, I'd come to the meeting woefully unprepared) to turn out to have such potential.

My original notion was a simple 'boy meets girl, boy loses girl, boy wins girl back' tale (hey, why mess with a proven formula?), the twist being that we'd see this story from two points of view – his and hers. As soon as I started the first draft I discovered the problems inherent in this idea: telling the story twice meant having to repeat myself, and no one likes watching repeats on TV, especially within the same programme. So this quickly evolved into a narrative device whereby characters would comment on events we'd just seen acted out – a technique that immediately became established as a *Cold Feet* style.

Someone once commented that a film is made three times: when it's written, when it's shot and when it's edited. As a writer it can be galling to see how the ideas you spilt blood, sweat and most of all tears to bring to the page are sometimes amended, refined or (goddammit!) just plain changed by the time they reach the screen. With *Cold Feet* I've been lucky that on the rare occasions when something turns up on screen different to how I'd envisaged or written it, it's generally better. (I say generally – you should hear the air turn blue when the change is, in my opinion, for the worse!)

The fact that the script improves as it moves from page to screen is a credit to everyone else working on the progamme. I don't just mean the producers, directors and the cast (and I don't intend to further sing their praises here as they more than adequately do that for themselves in the pages that follow) but the rest of the crew. A crew that's not interested, that's just going through the paces till 'wrap' is called for the day can do real damage to a show, not just because their shoddy work shows up on screen but also because their indifference filters through to everyone else. That's never been the case with *Cold Feet* because, across the board, I think we've all felt we've been contributing to something a bit special. Maybe that's why so many of the team who were on *Cold Feet* series one are still there as we're making series three (alternatively, it could be the money), among them associate producer David Meddick, film editor Tim Waddell, composer Mark Russell, production designer Chris Truelove, head of production Susy Liddell, location manager Ian Galley, first assistant director Simon Turner, second assistant director Elena Gabrilatsou, costume designer Joey Attawia, make-up supervisor Janet Horsfield, wardrobe supervisor Judith Wroe, sound recordist Nick Steer, boom operator Ben Brookes, casting director Michelle Smith, wardrobe assistant Roy Charters, script supervisor Helen Moran, camera grip Mike Fisher, lighting gaffer Dave Ratcliffe, electricians Len Holt, Gord Craig and Graham Heyes, production buyer Trevor Devoy, dressing props Roy Vivash and Alan Scholes and Actions Cars' Alan Eccleston.

What follows is a selection of some of the more memorable scenes from the pilot and the first two series, chosen by the key actors, the six directors, two executive producers, one press officer and me. Rather than try to agree a common list (which would have been impossible – as a group we can't even agree where to have lunch), each person has chosen their favourite scenes. Hopefully, these make sense even if you didn't happen to see that particular episode. (And anoraks who have the shows on video can trawl through comparing the scripts to the finished programmes. I admit I've done it.)

Finally, a personal thank you if I may. Writing thirteen hours of prime time drama was tough, but at times was probably harder on my family – so thanks to Lisa, Maggie and (latterly) Rachel for keeping me sane and keeping me going.

Mike Bullen
June 2000

Executive producer Andy Harries, controller of comedy and executive of film at Granada Television:

'We wanted to make a series about a very neglected part of the vast viewing public – people in their early- to mid-thirties. About three years ago there was very little comedy drama which reflected young people's lives. What we were interested in tapping into was people who were on the cusp of single life or living together – some just getting married or maybe having their first baby. We were very keen to try to develop a programme that tackled the issues and reflected the lifestyles, aspirations and problems of young professionals.

'The show was written with John Thomson in mind. John was in Mike Bullen's first TV work, *The Perfect Match,* which was made for ITV in 1995. Mike was working for the BBC World Service on a radio show about the cinema and he wrote *The Perfect Match* about a guy who proposed to his girlfriend in the middle of the FA Cup Final. An agent sent me the script speculatively, and I thought it was very fresh. Anyway, I sold it to ITV and we made it, and it did very well. Out of *The Perfect Match* grew *Cold Feet.* Also, it cemented the relationship between Mike and me. Because he wrote so well about his age group, that was the starting point for doing a series about people in their thirties.

'*Cold Feet* started out as just one couple, but I thought that we needed three. John Thomson had been working with me with Caroline Aherne and Steve Coogan. He is a fantastic comic and a very natural actor, so we knew we wanted to cast him for *Cold Feet.* He was the only one in place from the beginning. We cast Helen Baxendale because we liked her in *Cardiac Arrest* and I really thought she could do comedy. But when she came in, she said: "I don't know why I'm here because I can't do comedy." But I pointed out that *Cardiac Arrest* was really a drama with comedy in it. I had always liked Robert Bathurst from *Joking Apart* and Christine Langan, who produced the first two series but is now executive producer with me, found Fay Ripley and Hermione Norris, and championed Jimmy Nesbitt. Apart from Helen, it was pretty much an unknown cast at the time. This meant they didn't bring a lot of baggage with them, which was good

'One way in which we have kept the programme fresh is by choosing directors who have come from different disciplines. We have tended not to choose directors who have built up huge bodies of work. Christine has taken tremendous risks with directors who have often done very little and it is quite against the accepted law of television to hire relatively inexperienced directors to work on a major series like this. But we constantly wanted to push the style and allow directors to do their own thing.

'One of the best decisions we made early on was to set *Cold Feet* in Manchester. Mike set the first script in London, but it was Christine's idea that we should move it to Manchester. There were two basic advantages: firstly, it was a bit cheaper to film in Manchester and with Granada's facilities being there, it was a good opportunity to reduce the budget. More importantly, if we had filmed it in London, it might well have become that Islington/Camden/Primrose Hill type of North London thing with the Groucho Club and all that, which is rather alienating to everyone north of Watford. There is a certain self-satisfaction to London media life which we wanted to avoid, so when we started focusing on Manchester, it became a different proposition altogether and was much more reflective of any place, anywhere, any time. It was much more generic and less specific, yet its regionality gave it real strength and real roots, even though John Thomson is actually the only Mancunian in it. We also produce *The Royle Family*, and I see *The Royle Family* and *Cold Feet* as companion shows. They are very different, but also very similar. One is a working-class version of Manchester life and the other is a middle-class version of Manchester life. But both work because there is a huge element of truth in them.

'There's no doubt in my mind that what hired *Cold Feet* as a series was winning the Golden Rose of Montreux. The pilot show had gone out later than scheduled because ITV had just bought Formula 1, and the Grand Prix that day had overrun. So, instead of going out at 10 pm as planned, it went out at 10.40, which meant a huge number of people didn't see it. The ratings were around 3$\frac{1}{2}$ million and it picked up a smattering of reviews but, to be honest, it was a bit of a damp squib. We were all bitterly disappointed. The following morning, I said to Christine: "That's it – we'll never get a series now."

'But because ITV had so little comedy at the time, *Cold Feet* was entered for the Golden Rose of Montreux, something which had always been my dream to win. I remember when David Liddiment had first been appointed head of comedy at Granada, we had discussed winning the Golden Rose. The show received good word of mouth at the festival, but I still thought we had so little chance of winning that I actually left Montreux early. I flew back to Heathrow on the Monday morning and the winners were being announced in the middle of the afternoon. When I landed at Heathrow, there was a very large sign saying, "Andy Harries. STOP!" I flew back on the same plane I'd just arrived in and picked up my gong.

'David Liddiment was chairman of the jury that year and obviously was a huge fan of the show. And when he became network director of the ITV Centre, he finally commissioned a six-part series. BBC and Channel 4 also offered us a series and it has to be said that ITV were still extremely cautious about us. But they put us on a Sunday night, which is perfect for us. The traditional slot for a programme like ours on ITV on a Sunday night is 9 pm, which is known as the ironing slot because it is supposed to be undemanding. But the network didn't want *Cold Feet* to go out at 9 – they wanted it to go out at 10. In the end, David Liddiment found a compromise and put it out at 9.30. This gave a message to the audience that this is slightly different from what you would normally see, but stay with it. And fortunately, they did. The first series did pretty well, the second series did very well, and hopefully the third series will fare even better.'

Executive producer Christine Langan:

'It's an exciting time for a producer when you have a pilot script in your hand. *Cold Feet* was my first production and I was kind of scared, but in a thrilling way. Putting flesh on bones makes casting exciting, especially when you've got a large ensemble cast. All six characters were different, vibrant and needed a great deal of attention. I suppose I didn't have any cocky assumptions about how much weight – how much pull – we would have when it came to casting. I felt as if we were just a jumped-up little pilot from nowhere! In fact, the script was so beautifully written that actors loved it – probably more than we realized at the time. And now people are queuing up, hoping to be in *Cold Feet*.

'I had begged Mike Bullen to write a role with John Thomson in mind. John was in *The Perfect Match* and I know Mike was very impressed with John's natural comedy and didn't take much persuading to write a part that was suitable for him. Thankfully, John was up for it. Jimmy Nesbitt was suggested by Declan Lowney, who directed *Father Ted*, as well as the pilot and first two episodes of *Cold Feet*. Jimmy, too, was very keen. I was lucky to have a fantastic casting director, Kate Rhodes James. Kate, Declan and I met a lot of people. We'd invite them in and keep them for ages, chatting to them, getting to know them. Helen Baxendale became available halfway through the casting process. We were enchanted by her – she seemed perfect for the idolized Rachel. And when Helen and Jimmy read together, there was this unmistakable chemistry.

'Jenny was proving the hardest character to cast. Off the page, she read as somewhat hectoring and naggy, and most of the actresses we had in went for the predictable approach of being finger-wagging, complaining and whining. Then Fay Ripley came in. I didn't really know her work, but she did the most unusual reading of Jenny. She just bowled us over by doing this complete left-field approach. Some of it was quite strange, actually, but it was really compelling and inherently funny. There was attitude and wit in everything she did. We knew that she'd be able to tell Pete off without sounding as if she was moaning.

'And we looked at a tremendous number of people for David and Karen. But those two fell into place with the chemistry between Robert Bathurst and Hermione Norris. So what we had going for us was three really strong couples, as well as six strong individuals. All six never met in the pilot but as the series has developed, we've found ourselves with a scenario rather like the famous "I look down on him ..." sketch in *The Frost Report* with John Cleese, Ronnie Barker and Ronnie Corbett. There is an element of that with our boys in that they are very different from each other. Pete

Cold Feet – the best bits...

and Adam clown around and have an affinity with each other, but all three occupy very distinct territory. I think that's the beauty of the six of them – they are all really their own people. All the girls are brilliant, sexy and attractive, yet they are all really different and distinct so that you know what you are dealing with.

'I see the actors as individual guardians of their role. They have individually matured, taken on those roles and made them their own. No one else knows their character from their position, which is a crucial factor. Mike and I can argue the toss about how well we know those characters, but neither of us can know them from the inside, which is a valuable perspective. Up until this third series, Mike has written every episode and understandably, he is very adamant about a lot of his work. He is a superb writer and consequently, we have never been cavalier with the script. Sometimes people might individualize the odd line, but we are respectful as to how much they get changed beyond the read-through.

'I have hired directors on the basis that they will give their all. I have used very ambitious directors who will make their two-hour bite at this cherry their feature film. They each have movie ambitions, they are hungry and they need and want this opportunity to showcase their talents. They are not jobbing directors. And I think this helps to give *Cold Feet* that certain freshness.'

Director Declan Lowney:

'I was doing Father Ted when my agent rang me and told me about this new pilot. So they sent me the script and, to be honest, I didn't like it much at first. I thought the characters were very smug, but when I read it again I could see that it was quite clever. I suddenly thought these are like people I know, so I started to picture my friends and it became a much more interesting proposition. Then when you thought about casting and about the sort of actors you'd put into it, and when you saw it less about cliché casting, you suddenly saw its possibilities. So I met up with Christine and we just got on very well. She's very bright and we clicked straight away. My background was sit-com, but I wanted to do drama, and Christine was pushing at Granada to get in someone a bit different to direct *Cold Feet*.

'With the casting, John Thomson was already part of the package and I think he is brilliant anyway. I'd met Jimmy Nesbitt through a friend and I got him in for casting. We loved him and he loved it, and it just clicked. And we've got on extremely well ever since. Jimmy's part could have gone so very wrong and been so smug. You don't want to like Adam, but Jimmy makes him likeable – he brings something very special to the role. He was a joy to work with and made life very easy for me. He is very responsive. If you can't think of how to do a particular scene, he will come up with a suggestion, which is a terrific help to a director. I remember seeing him in a Persil commercial and thinking: this guy is absolutely brilliant. He's got such a wonderfully expressive face.

'Fay Ripley came in and just blew us away. She was so real, I believed in her completely. It wasn't like acting – it was just brilliant comic timing. And I think it helped that she reminds me of a friend of mine.

'We first saw Hermione Norris for the part of Rachel, but didn't feel she was right for it. I thought of her for the part of Karen instead because Karen is like David – upmarket, posh, likeable and personable – and, to tell the truth, Hermione is posh, too.

'Robert Bathurst is great as David, the posh twit. David is a terrific fall guy but if anything goes wrong, it is never his fault. It's always someone else's fault. Yet somehow you can't help liking him because Robert brings a real vulnerability to the part.

'There was something very special about Helen Baxendale when she came to the casting. I'd seen her a few times in *Cardiac Arrest* and thought she was excellent in that. Helen's sweet, but definitely in her own world. That's what I love about her.

'So we did the pilot and had a ball doing it. I hadn't ever done anything like it before – 12 days to shoot and a week to talk about it. I'm very open to ideas; I like to get the actors involved and they love that. So everyone enjoyed it. There was a buzz about the whole thing and even the crew were laughing, which is always a good sign.

'One of my favourite scenes from the pilot is where Karen bursts in on David at the seminar and demands that they get a nanny. I shot the first part on a long lens in a street in Manchester, with six extras criss-crossing in front of Karen. They are all smartly dressed in suits and coats, and she's in a grubby T-shirt and slippers, with a tea towel over her shoulder and the baby on one arm. You see a look on her face and you wonder: Jesus, what is she going to do? She goes into that room where David's giving his talk, and she's scary. He brilliantly tries to turn it around by pretending that she's a talented actress and it's all part of a role play, but she still manages to have the last word. It's a really good piece of writing and a lovely performance from Hermione and Robert. There is great chemistry between them in *Cold Feet*. He could be unlikeable, but he's not, and she could be cold, but instead she is very warm and accessible. So although they are dead posh, you don't mind.'

Robert Bathurst (David):

'The seminar scene was the first day's filming I did on *Cold Feet*. In the pilot, David was set up as a post-Thatcherite boo-boy to represent all that is evil about materialism and, as such, I was always on the lookout that he wasn't wholly two-dimensional. He's opinionated, but has spectacularly bad judgement, which makes him very vulnerable. However, dear old David does have admirable qualities and this scene shows that, while he is fundamentally dishonest, he is also quick-witted and can think on his feet. It is a funny scene – a farcical scene – and one where, as in the best farcical moments, loss of reputation is all. He was facing loss of reputation and I'm afraid the risk of upsetting his wife was way down on his list of priorities. In the same sequence, I added in a line where I asked my secretary to fetch sugar for my coffee. Mike Bullen said he warmed to David after that and told me he got some idea of the true potential horror of the character from that line.'

SCENE 79A SUMMER EVENING DAY 20
SET   EXT BUSY STREETS

KAREN: JOSH:

KAREN BATTLES THROUGH THE STREETS AGAINST A TIDAL FLOW OF
PEOPLE.

SCENE 80 SUMMER EVENING 20
SET   INT CONFERENCE ROOM

DAVID: KAREN: JOSHUA:
GRADUATE TRAINEES N/S:

DAVID STANDS BEFORE A GROUP OF GRADUATE TRAINEES, THE
SLIGHT MAJORITY OF WHOM ARE MEN. BEHIND HIM IS A
WHITEBOARD ON WHICH, UNDER THE HEADING "NEGOTIATING
SKILLS", HAVE BEEN WRITTEN 4 BULLET POINTS: 1. BOTTOM
LINE; 2. PERSEVERANCE; 3. COUNTERMEASURES; 4.
ULTIMATUM. THE STUDENTS TAKE NOTES.

> DAVID:
> So, to recap. (HE INDICATES EACH POINT) Be clear
> about your bottom line, settle for nothing less,
> have counter-arguments ready to disarm your
> opponent, and if all else fails, issue an
> ultimatum.

THE DOOR BURSTS OPEN AND KAREN SWEEPS INTO THE ROOM.

> KAREN:
> David, we're going to get a nanny!

DAVID TURNS, SLACKJAWED AT THIS UNEXPECTED INTERRUPTION.

> DAVID:
> Karen! I'm giving a seminar.

> KAREN:
> I don't care. I want a nanny!

THE CLASS STIRS AT THIS UNANTICIPATED INTERRUPTION.

> DAVID:
> (A HISSED ASIDE) We'll discuss it later.

> KAREN:
> We'll discuss it now!

> DAVID:
> (STEELY) I am not prepared to leave my child with
> some woman who, for all we know, could have a
> history of mental illness.

> KAREN:
> We let your sister babysit. Besides, we'll go to
> a reputable agency and check references.

> DAVID:
> And you're happy, are you, to have Josh grow up
> thinking of someone else as his Mummy?

AN INTAKE OF BREATH FROM THE WOMEN STUDENTS, SHOCKED AT
THIS CHEAP SHOT; THE MEN TUT AT KAREN'S APPARENT
NEGLIGENCE.

KAREN:
(COOLLY) He'll be in no doubt who his Mummy is, though you're so rarely there, he could be forgiven for thinking it's a one parent family.

MORE REACTION FROM THE AUDIENCE, THIS TIME AGAINST DAVID.

DAVID:
(PLAYING TO THE AUDIENCE) And where am I? At work providing for my family. And now you want me to provide for a nanny as well.

THE MEN MURMUR IN HIS SUPPORT; KAREN APPEALS TO THE WOMEN.

KAREN:
I can go back to work part-time which will more than meet the expense.

A BEAT. DAVID IS AWARE HE'S LOSING THIS ARGUMENT.

DAVID:

(WITH FINALITY) No. I'm fundamentally opposed to the idea. I will not share my house with a nanny.

KAREN:
(STEELY-EYED) David, unless we get a nanny, you won't have to share your house at all. Because I'll leave and I'll take Josh with me.

SHOCK FROM THE AUDIENCE. ALL EYES ON DAVID, WHO NERVOUSLY CONSIDERS WHETHER SHE'S SERIOUS AND CONCLUDES SHE IS.

DAVID:
(CAVING IN) Alright, we'll get a nanny.

THE WOMEN IN THE AUDIENCE CLAP; KAREN ACKNOWLEDGES THEIR SUPPORT AS SHE AND JOSH LEAVE. DAVID GATHERS HIMSELF AS THE AUDIENCE SETTLE, SOMEWHAT ENJOYING HIS EMBARRASSMENT.

DAVID:
(WITH A KNOWING SMILE) The purpose of that role-playing exercise was to illustrate (INDICATES THE WHITEBOARD) the four key points of successful negotiation. (THE AUDIENCE WONDERS. WERE THEY BEING FOOLED?) Yes, I know you thought it was for real. Sorry to disappoint you.   That lady was an an actress.

THE AUDIENCE RELAXES AND APPLAUDS DAVID'S LECTURING SKILLS. THE DOOR OPENS AND KAREN POPS HER HEAD ROUND.

KAREN:
(SWEETLY) Oh, darling, I've locked myself out. Can I borrow your keys?

DAVID'S SELF-SATISFIED SMILE MELTS FROM HIS FACE.

CUT TO

Writer Mike Bullen:

'The *Cold Feet* characters are all based on people I know – friends of mine. In the pilot, Adam was based on me because at that stage I was drifting from one failed relationship to another. By the first series, I'd met my wife and we'd had our first child, so I was more like Pete, grappling with the horrors of parenthood. Now I'm more like David – self-satisfied and smug, a father of two, and wondering where it all went wrong!

'So in the original, Adam was me and Pete was my best mate, whom I have known since I was 11. Jenny was actually the wife of another friend. The characteristic I took from her was that she has a mind of her own and a tongue in her head, and she doesn't mind using either. David and Karen were based on a married couple and he really is in the City. And he called his kid "Junior Sausage", which I got David to call Josh! But the real David is much nicer – he's not a buffoon or pompous, but they do live quite well. The real Karen is like her screen counterpart – stylish and attractive. As for Rachel, she is a combination of ex-girlfriends and Cameron Diaz – so, ex-girlfriends and fantasy girlfriends. I hadn't met my wife at the point I wrote Rachel ...

'The driving force behind *Cold Feet* was that we didn't think there was anything on TV that spoke to our generation in an intelligent way. Christine Langan and I are both keen on good American television and tend to look towards the States for ideas. The pilot was originally just the central characters, Adam and Rachel. Then Andy Harries said that if we wanted this to be a series, we needed more characters. So in the pilot the other characters' stories are a bit tacked on. Then, as it moved into a series, it became a true ensemble piece.

'I suppose the scene which most people remember from the pilot was where Adam proves his undying love for Rachel by serenading her in the street outside her flat, stark naked apart from a rose up his bum. Although quite a few incidents were taken from my life, I never did anything like that. Yet, it was about the first thing that came to me for the pilot. I've always been quite keen on the idea of big romantic gestures, but for them to really work on screen they have to be within the realms of possibility. I think a rose up the bum is stretching things a bit, but if you are really keen and desperately in love, I wouldn't put it past a lot of men to do that. The nearest I got to making such a gesture was a long, long time ago. It didn't cause me any embarassment, but it was quite a romantic thing to do. I was about 18, still living at home in Birmingham, and there was this girl I was keen on who had gone to Southampton University. Rather than just ring her up and ask her for a date, I decided it would be quite romantic to drive down there with a bunch of roses and ask her for a date. And she would be bound to say, "Why are you in town?" And I would say, "I've just driven down and I'm going back now." So I drove down. I didn't even know if she would be there, so it was pretty stupid to go all that way, but luckily she was, and she was duly impressed and we started going out. So that was where the roses came in, although I concede that it's a bit of a leap from that to shoving them up your arse!

'Jimmy Nesbitt had to be practically naked for filming that scene. He wasn't totally naked – he wore a very small pouch. When you are a writer, you don't consider the actors' sensibilities, but I don't think Jimmy minded too much. The production manager was more nervous. He said that if any of the neighbours were to complain to the police, they could close us down because technically we could have been guilty of breaching the peace or offending public morality. So he was keen that Jimmy should wear a dressing-gown whenever he didn't need to be naked. But I think the locals loved it, to be honest. The only time we used a stuntman was when Jimmy gets thrown out of the house onto the pavement. Unfortunately, the stunt guy was about four stone heavier and four inches shorter than Jimmy. He only appears on screen for around five seconds, but if you watch closely you can see that Adam has shrunk and put on a lot of weight.'

Director Declan Lowney:

'Since Cold Feet was originally set in London, the rose scene was going to be set in Chelsea ... on a double-decker bus. It started out on paper with Rachel on a balcony and Adam passing by on the bus, and then the police came. It was a bit more farcical. I did three or four drafts on the scene with Mike and we ended up shooting it on location with Rachel seeing Adam through a window. The other thing that changed was that originally Adam was going to be singing Nilsson's "Without You". I didn't want to use it. I thought it was a bit naff, but Mike was pushing for it. However, we couldn't get clearance for that song but we knew we could for Cole Porter's "I've Got You Under My Skin". So we went for that instead and it was a funny song to do because of the rose association. Jimmy sings it beautifully – he loves singing! Any excuse!

'He was great doing the rose scene. It took about two hours in all and he was near

Cold Feet – the best bits...

naked most of the time. He had no qualms about it, but I find that kind of stuff hard to do. I get very embarassed having to say: "Can we see a shot of your arse now, please?" But Jimmy doesn't. There were police around whilst we were filming, but there were no problems. But that was when we were an unknown pilot show. It would be trickier shooting something like that in Manchester now that the show has become big.'

James Nesbitt (Adam):

'I suppose the rose up the bum is the enduring image of *Cold Feet* – it's the scene which people still talk about four years on. I was nervous about doing it, but the anticipation was worse than the reality, even though it was much more open than I'd imagined. It wasn't a closed set and was very exposed to the public, so I had all these people hanging out of windows, watching me. It was a real rose – with the thorns removed – which was taped to my backside. All I wore was this pouch, which was fitted by a very butch Australian dresser. So I think it was worse for him than me! Irrespective of the cold and the embarrassment, I feel privileged that I was the one who did it. If that is my acting legacy, then so be it ...'

The Scripts

```
SCENE  85 SUMMER EVENING DAY 20
SET   INT SIMON'S FLAT

RACHEL:  SIMON:  ADAM:

SIMON OPENS THE DOOR TO FIND ADAM STANDING THERE, SLIGHTLY
DISHEVELLED.

                    ADAM:
          (TAKEN ABACK BY SIMON'S SIZE) Christ, you're big.
          (DOUBLE-CHECKING) Simon, right?

                    SIMON:
          Yes?

ADAM TAKES A DEEP BREATH THEN BARGES HIS WAY IN, A REPEAT
OF THE PREVIOUS SCENE.

                    ADAM:
          Alright, where is she?

                    RACHEL:
          (FROM THE LOUNGE)  Adam?

                    SIMON:
          Oi!  You can't just barge in here!

ADAM THROWS HIMSELF INTO THE LOUNGE, WHERE RACHEL HAS RISEN
FROM HER CHAIR.  A MOMENT LATER, SIMON ALSO APPEARS.
```

RACHEL:
What are you doing here?!

ADAM:
I had to see you!

SIMON:
(TO RACHEL) Is this the computer salesman?

ADAM:
(TO SIMON; AS IN "I'LL HAVE YOU KNOW") Systems
analyst.

RACHEL:
(TO NO-ONE IN PARTICULAR) Whatever that is.

ADAM:
(TO RACHEL, THROWN AWAY) I'll explain it
sometime. Look, I want a recount. You
can't pick him. I love you too much.

SIMON:
We don't have to listen to this!

HE ATTEMPTS TO MAN-HANDLE ADAM OUT OF THE ROOM. A SCUFFLE
BEGINS. SIMON'S SUPERIOR STRENGTH TELLS; ADAM IS DRAGGED
OUT INTO THE HALL, AND GRADUALLY TOWARDS THE FRONT DOOR,
WHICH IS STILL OPEN.

ADAM:
(AS THEY GRAPPLE) We weren't drifting apart. I
just scared myself by being so far in.
But we're right for each other! And
I'm ready to hang my shirts in your wardrobe! If
you'll let ...

FROM THE HALLWAY, WE SEE SIMON CHUCK ADAM OUT OF
THE FRONT DOOR.

CUT TO

SCENE 86 SUMMER EVENING DAY 20
SET EXT SIMON'S FLAT

SIMON: ADAM:

SIMON SUCCEEDS IN THROWING ADAM DOWN THE OUTSIDE STEPS.

ADAM:
(AS HE FALLS) Meeeeeeeeee!

ADAM ARRIVES IN A HEAP AT THE BOTTOM OF THE STEPS, AND
LIES ON HIS BACK LIKE AN UPTURNED BEETLE.

ADAM:
I'm okay! It's all right, I'm okay!

SIMON SLAMS THE DOOR. ADAM WINCES. IT'S CLEAR HE'S NOT
ENTIRELY ALRIGHT.

CUT TO

SCENE 87 SUMMER EVENING DAY 20
SET INT SIMON'S LOUNGE

RACHEL: SIMON: ADAM:

RACHEL IS STANDING, QUIETLY SOBBING, UPSET BY THE WHOLE
INCIDENT. SIMON HOLDS HER TO HIM, AND GENTLY STROKES HER
HAIR. SHE RESTS HER HEAD ON HIS SHOULDER.

                    SIMON:
          Hey, hey, come on. Don't cry. It's over.

FROM OUTSIDE DRIFTS ADAM'S VOICE, SINGING "WITHOUT YOU".

                    ADAM:
          "When I think about tomorrow, and I think of all
          my sorrow how I had you there and then I let you
          go and now, it's only fair that I should let you
          know..."

SIMON LOOKS TOWARDS THE WINDOW.

                    SIMON:
          Jesus! What now!

SIMON CROSSES TO THE WINDOW & LOOKS OUT. DOWN BELOW,
ACROSS THE STREET, STANDS ADAM, STARK NAKED, STILL SINGING
"WITHOUT YOU". RACHEL JOINS SIMON AT THE WINDOW JUST AS
ADAM, THROWING HIS ARMS WIDE, REACHES THE BIG CHORUS.
PASSERS-BY STARE.

                    ADAM:
          (GOING FOR IT) "Can't live, li-i-i-i-ive, if
          living is without you..." (ETC)

SEEING RACHEL LOOKING OUT, ADAM SPINS ROUND TO REVEAL A
ROSE STOLEN FROM THE OLD LADY'S GARDEN LODGED IN HIS BUM.

                    SIMON:
          (WITH FINALITY) I'm going to put a stop to this
          once and for all!

HE TURNS & MARCHES TOWARDS THE DOOR. RACHEL TRIES TO HOLD
HIM BACK, AND FAILS.

                    RACHEL:
          Simon! No!

CUT TO

```
SCENE  87A SUMMER EVENING DAY 20
SET  EXT SIMON'S HOUSE

RACHEL:  ADAM:  SIMON:

RACHEL APPEARS AT THE WINDOW AND URGENTLY POINTS TOWARDS
THE DOOR.  ADAM STOPS SINGING, SMILES AND GIVES HER AN
ENCOURAGING THUMBS UP.  HE STARTS TO MOVE TOWARDS THE DOOR
AS IT IS FLUNG OPEN TO REVEAL SIMON STANDING THERE LIKE
JAKE LAMOTTA.  SIMON ADOPTS THE CLASSIC KARATE STANCE.
ADAM STOPS DEAD IN HIS TRACKS.  HE MOUTHS ...

                    ADAM:
          Oh shit!

... AND DECIDES A RUNNER IS THE BEST OPTION.  HE TURNS AND
RUNS AWAY FROM SIMON.

CUT TO:
```

The Antenatal Class Scene, Series One, Episode One

Writer Mike Bullen:

'When I was writing series one, we had recently had our first child so a lot of the emotion during the birthing business and the birthing class was based on my own experience. Maggie was a month premature, so we never finished the classes. We never even did the tour of the hospital – we just went in. In the class I went to, there was a quiz, where we were given callipers, forceps and a suction cap to play with, and we had to say what we thought these were for. It was quite amusing. The women looked absolutely horrified because they knew these instruments of torture were going to be used on them, whereas it brought out my competitive spirit. I was determined not to be the most stupid man in the class. It's the same with Pete – he has mugged up on everything and knows all the answers. It's that competitive steak that men often have.'

Executive Producer Christine Langan:

'The antenatal scene always makes me laugh, with Jenny reflecting the fear that women always fear around childbirth and Pete gurning terribly, the eagerness of the expectant father. I love the bit where he demonstrates the dangers of the umbilical cord by hanging himself with his tie.'

The Scripts

```
SCENE  45 INT
SET   ANTENATAL CLINIC
NIGHT 7  1930

PETE:
JENNY:
Antenatal Midwife:
Prospective Dad:
Other couples n/s:

PETE AND JENNY AND A NUMBER OF OTHER COUPLES (PLUS A SINGLE
WOMAN) LISTEN AS A MIDWIFE GIVES A LECTURE ON THE
BIRTHING PROCESS. THE AUDIENCE PASS AROUND BIRTHING
IMPLEMENTS - A VENTOUSE SUCTION CAP ETC.  (JENNY LOOKS WITH
FOREBODING AT A PAIR OF FORCEPS SHE'S HOLDING).  THE
AUDIENCE ARE ALL VERY RELAXED (SITTING CASUALLY, DRINKING
COFFEE, ETC)  SAVE ONE - PETE, WHO LISTENS ATTENTIVELY,
TAKING COPIOUS NOTES.

                    MIDWIFE:

    In most cases within a day or two of the birth you'll

    be discharged and allowed to take your baby home.

PETE MAKES A NOTE OF THIS.  JENNY WATCHES HIM, SHE CAN'T
BELIEVE HOW SERIOUSLY HE'S TAKING ALL THIS.
```

Cold Feet – the best bits...

JENNY:

(ASIDE TO PETE, SARCASTICALLY) I don't think we'll

forget to take her home.

PETE SMILES AT HER, UNAWARE THAT SHE'S MAKING A DIG.

MIDWIFE:

Right, to end, just for a bit of fun, I thought we'd

have a little quiz.

PETE LOOKS ENTHUSIASTICALLY AT JENNY AND SHIFTS IN HIS SEAT
LIKE THE KID AT SCHOOL WHO WAS ALWAYS EAGER TO SHOW OFF
THEIR KNOWLEDGE IN TESTS.

MIDWIFE:

Just call out if you know the answer. Okay, question

one, how wide is the cervix when fully dilated?

THERE'S NO PAUSE BETWEEN HER ASKING THE QUESTION AND PETE
ANSWERING IT.

PETE:

(IN ONE BREATH) Ten centimetres or four inches.

MIDWIFE:

(TAKEN ABACK BY THE VEHEMENCE AND SPEED OF PETE'S

ANSWER) Yes very good. Erm, when the top of the

baby's head is visible...

PETE:

(INTERRUPTING) It's called "crowning"!

MIDWIFE:

Er, yes. That wasn't actually going to be the

question... (JENNY LOOKS EMBARRASSED TO BE WITH PETE)

When the head crowns, should you push?

PETE IS BEATEN TO IT BY ANOTHER OF THE MEN IN THE GROUP.

PROSPECTIVE DAD:

No, because if the head's born too quickly, the

mother's skin might tear.

**AMENDED 18/02/98

*PETE MOUTHS THE WORD "BASTARD".** JENNY LOOKS AT HIM IN
DISBELIEF AT HIS COMPTITIVENESS.

MIDWIFE:

Very good. Erm, maybe we could let one of the Mums

answer the next one. When the baby's head appears, the

midwife will check the umbilical cord. Why?

PETE LOOKS ENCOURAGINGLY AT JENNY, WHO JUST STARES BLANKLY
BACK AT HIM, REFUSING TO BE DRAWN INTO HIS CHILDISH GAME.
PETE FIDGETS AND NUDGES HER "COME ON!", THEN MIMICS CHOKING
AS A NOOSE TIGHTENS ROUND HIS NECK.

MIDWIFE:

Anyone?

CAUGHT OFF GUARD, PETE IS AGAIN BEATEN TO IT BY THE OTHER
KNOWLEDGABLE BLOKE.

CAUGHT OFF GUARD, PETE IS AGAIN BEATEN TO IT BY THE OTHER
KNOWLEDGABLE BLOKE.

PROSPECTIVE DAD:

To ensure it isn't looped around the baby's neck.

THE PROSPECTIVE DAD SMILES AT PETE TRIUMPHANTLY. ANNOYED,
PETE TURNS TO JENNY AND GIVES HER A LOOK TO INDICATE HIS
DISAPPOINTMENT IN HER. SHE REGARDS HIM COOLLY - PATHETIC!

CUT TO

Writer Mike Bullen:

'One of my favourite scenes from the first series is in episode one, where Jenny expresses her fears about having the baby. Pete is repacking Jenny's bag for the hospital and for the first time, she confesses that she is really scared about this. She throws him up against the wardrobe, pins him against it and says: "I'm scared. Shit scared."

'Well, that scene was written while they were filming, simply because the script was too short. Before you write for television, you always presume that scripts are shot exactly as they are intended – to that length – but in fact, it's nothing like that. I'd finished the script, everyone was happy with it, but it was coming in a few minutes short. So we had to fill it, otherwise viewers would have had to suffer a lot more adverts. I said to Christine: "I've written the story. I don't know what else there is to do." She said: "We haven't yet seen any vulnerability on Jenny's part. Couldn't we see a scene where she expresses that?"

'I could see what she was getting at, so I wrote the scene. And I was pleased with the result because I managed to get some humour in as well. Jenny gets angry with Pete and says, "Forget my nightie, forget my cardigan, forget my toothbrush" ... and he suddenly remembers that he's forgotten to pack Jenny's toothbrush and says "Toothbrush!" That's what causes her to throw him against the wardrobe. I'm pleased because that line always gets a laugh. That is what *Cold Feet* is trying to be about – comedy and drama at the same time. The other reason I like that scene is that the rest of the episode is amusing and light, and that is the first moment when you suddenly think, "Hey, it's a bit more serious." Yet, it was tacked on simply because they were short.

'The other thing about episode one is that it gave me my only speaking part in *Cold Feet*. I did brief cameos in a few of the episodes, but this was the only one where I was given a line. I was a bloke on the phone and I had to say "Seven what?" I didn't deliver it well. It took quite a few takes ...

'In episode two, I was a nosy neighbour, who saw Adam trying to hang the child from the washing line; in episode four, I was the husband of the Japanese woman at the christening; and in episode three, I did my first-ever nude scene! It's where David is confessing to Adam that he has a problem with impotence. Adam is quite gleeful on hearing this, but David asks him whether he has any advice he can offer and that sets up Adam to go and talk to Pete. And that's where the confusion sets in as people jump to the conclusion that it's Adam with the impotence problem. Anyway, because I'd been doing a few Hitchcock-like appearances, I thought it would be fun to do a nude scene – just out of interest to see what filming a nude scene was like. It was filmed in the squash court showers and it was fascinating. For the first two minutes you feel really self-conscious because there are 30 people – half of whom are women – all standing around fully-clothed, while you're standing there starkers. But after that, you forget you are naked except that you feel more self-conscious because they give you a pair of slippers and, if you are naked apart from slippers, you actually feel much more naked than if you haven't got anything on. Added to which, you look ridiculous. Unfortunately, my scene was cut. They said it was because the camera lens kept steaming up in the showers, but I think it was because I only had a small part ...'

Director Declan Lowney:

'After the pilot show had won the Golden Rose, I'd gone to Ireland to do a film with Mia Farrow and Terence Stamp. I'd moved over to Dublin with my girlfriend Jenny and our son Danny. The film was supposed to shoot in October and *Cold Feet* was going into a series in the January. Christine rang me to ask whether I'd like to do the first two episodes but because of the film, I had to say no, which was disappointing. But then a week before shooting was due to begin, it collapsed. The backers pulled out. At the same time, Jenny, who had been six months pregnant with twins, was taken ill and the twins died. It was like the bottom had fallen out of my world. We were away from home and, although I'm Irish, we were in a strange place. It took so long to recover. So when Christine asked me again whether I wanted to do the first two episodes, I said yes.

'The whole birthing episode was very emotional for me because of all the stuff I'd just gone through, but I think the comedy aspect helped me get over it in a way. The scene where Fay, as Jenny, admits her fears for the first time came about as a result of a conversation I had with my girlfriend one night. We were talking about the things that used to happen the first time she was pregnant and she said that people don't realize how incredibly alone you feel as an expectant mother. Sometimes, even your partner doesn't realize it. So I talked to Christine and Mike about it and we put the scene in at the end of part two.

'It's a fabulous scene. Pete is pissed and completely misunderstands her. He fusses around her like men do because they can't see the bigger picture when all she wants is a hug. And I love the bit where she throws him against the wardrobe. We only rehearsed it on the day and, at the end of the rehearsal, there were tears coming down my eyes.'

Fay Ripley (Jenny):

'My favourite scene to act was where Jenny admitted to being scared about what was happening to her body. It was very well written – Mike's a very clever writer. On the day we filmed it, one of the members of the crew, who was heavily pregnant and about to give birth, burst into tears and had to leave the set. She was empathizing with Jenny. She was scared, too, about having her first baby. I particularly enjoyed the bit where I pinned John to the wardrobe. In fact, I asked for that to be shot again and again even though I believe John was perfectly happy with the first take ...'

The Scripts

```
SCENE  57A INT
SET  PETE & JENNY'S HOUSE - BEDROOM
NIGHT 8  2335
                          **NEW SCENE ISSUED 03/03/98

JENNY:
PETE:

JENNY SITS ON THE BED AS PETE PACKS HER AN OVERNIGHT BAG FOR
HER HOSPITAL STAY.  WATCHING THESE PREPARATIONS BRINGS HOME
TO HER THE IMMEDIACY AND (MORE IMPORTANTLY) THE ENORMITY OF
WHAT SHE'S FACING.  PETE BUSIES ABOUT, TAKING CLOTHES OUT OF
CUPBOARDS - HE HOLDS UP A JUMPER.

                    PETE:

    Can you still fit into this?

                    JENNY:

    (WITHOUT ENTHUSIASM)  Barely.

THAT'S GOOD ENOUGH FOR PETE.  HE CAREFULLY FOLDS IT ON THE
BED, AVOIDING CREASES, THEN ADDS IT TO THE SUITCASE WHICH
ALREADY CONTAINS KNICKERS, TOWELS, SLIPPERS, ETC.
```

Cold Feet – the best bits...

JENNY:

Look, can't we go to bed? There'll be time for that when my waters break.

PETE:

You won't want to be bothered with it then. (PETE CONSULTS THE CHECKLIST ON PAGE 242 OF "CONCEPTION, PREGNANCY & BIRTH" BY MIRIAM STOPPARD) Where's your maternity bra?

JENNY:

I'm wearing it.

PETE GIVES HER A LOOK - "DON'T BE DIFFICULT".

JENNY:

(RELUCTANTLY) Top drawer.

PETE FETCHES ONE, ADDING IT TO THE PILE OF CLOTHES, THEN AGAIN BURIES HIS HEAD IN MIRIAM.

**NEW SCENE ISSUED 03/03/98

JENNY:

Pete?

PETE:

(WITHOUT LOOKING UP) Hmmm?

JENNY:

(LOOKING AT CLOTHES - FEARFULLY) It's getting close now.

PETE:

(ABSENTLY) Hmm.

HE TAKES MORE CLOTHES FROM THE CUPBOARD AND ADDS THEM TO THE SUITCASE. JENNY GETS OFF THE BED.

JENNY:

(AN EDGE TO HER VOICE) Look, will you stop doing that?

PETE:

(OFF-HAND, FAILING TO NOTICE THE EDGE IN HER VOICE)

You'll thank me in the long run. (HOLDS UP TWO

DRESSING GOWNS FROM THE BACK OF THE WARDROBE) Blue or

green?

JENNY SNATCHES THE NEARER DRESSING GOWN OUT OF PETE'S HANDS,
WANTING HIM TO STOP PACKING.

JENNY:

No!!

PETE SHRUGS, AND FOLDING THE OTHER DRESSING GOWN, ADDS IT TO
THE SUITCASE. JENNY RIPS IF FROM THE SUITCASE AND FLINGS IT
ASIDE. A COUPLE OF PAIRS OF KNICKERS GO FLYING AS WELL.

JENNY:

I said stop it! I'm not ready!!

PETE:

(RETRIEVING KNICKERS AND GOING TO RE-PACK THEM) Jen,

love...

NEW SCENE ISSUED 03/03/98

JENNY BEGINS TO GET A BIT BERSERK. SHE RIPS THE PANTIES
FROM PETE'S HANDS AND FLINGS THEM ASIDE, THEN STARTS
THROWING OUT EVERYTHING HE'S PACKED INTO THE BAG. KNICKERS,
NIGHTDRESSES, BREAST PADS, SANITARY TOWELS GO FLYING ACROSS
THE ROOM.

JENNY:

(HYSTERICALLY) You're driving me crazy! Forget my

nighties! Forget my knickers! Forget my toothbrush!

PETE:

(BUTTING IN, REMEMBERING) Oh, I've forgotten your

toothbrush!

PETE MAKES AS IF TO GO TO THE BATHROOM TO FETCH THE
TOOTHBRUSH. HE DOESN'T EVEN MAKE IT OUT OF THE ROOM. JENNY
FLINGS HIM AGAINST A WARDROBE, PINNING HIM THERE, AND
STARING AT HIM BREATHING HEAVILY, A WOMAN ON THE VERGE...
PETE LOOKS AT HER SHOCKED, AND SLIGHTLY SCARED.

PETE:

(NERVOUSLY) You all right, love?

JENNY RELEASES HER HOLD ON PETE.

JENNY:

Oh, Pete. Don't you understand?!

A BEAT; NO, HE DOESN'T.

JENNY:

I'm scared. I'm scared shitless. I'm going to have a

baby.

PETE DOESN'T KNOW WHAT TO DO.

PETE:

(LIMPLY) I know. (BEAT, LAMELY) But I don't know

what to do about it.

JENNY:

(IMPLORINGLY) Just hold me, Pete.

HE TAKES HER IN HIS ARMS AND HUGS HER. ALL THE FEAR THAT'S
BEEN WELLING UP INSIDE JENNY BURSTS FORTH. SHE SOBS IN HIS
ARMS. HE HUGS HER TIGHTLY. THEY CLING TO EACH OTHER FOR
DEAR LIFE.

CUT TO

END OF ACT TWO

Director Declan Lowney:

'I've got two children now – Danny, born before the twins died and Ted, born afterwards. Ted is named after Father Ted because the day after we found out that Jen was pregnant again, Dermot Morgan died. It was the day we were shooting the *Cold Feet* scene in episode one, where Adam is on the tram on the way to the hospital. The news of Dermot's death had been on the radio that morning and I was the only one on the crew who didn't know. Jenny waited until lunch-time to tell me. It was all so sudden, very tragic. I couldn't believe it. I hadn't worked on the last series of Father Ted because I was working on the movie, but I had seen Dermot the week before and he was very, very tired. It had been the end of a very long schedule – it's hard going, shooting sit-coms. So we decided to call our second son Ted – we didn't want to call him Dermot!

'So all of the scenes in that episode have strong memories for me. The scene where Rachel drove her Mini (although actually, it was a stuntman rather than Helen Baxendale at the wheel) across the golf course to tell Pete that Jenny was in labour was shot at a big posh golf course outside Manchester. In the script, it was a golf buggy but somebody came up with the brilliant idea of making it Rachel's Mini. And since the car was red, it stood out really well on the green golf course. The golf club were understandably very precious about their course and we had to be very careful not to get the car anywhere near the greens. So when David and Pete are putting, the car might look close, but in actual fact we used a long lens so it was quite a long way away. We managed to do two or three takes and if you look at the shots, you can see the tyre marks from the previous takes. I'm amazed we got away with it. Even if we had been able to do more takes, there wasn't really the time. You can't hang around anywhere too long because it's bloody hard work sticking to the schedule. Twelve days for 52 minutes' television is four to five minutes a day, and that's a lot. The time just goes.

'I thought John Thomson's reaction in that scene is great. The camera moves in on them and it freezes. It must be some kind of drama. OH, MY GOD! And David is so patronizing towards him when they are playing golf. I love that bit where he stands behind Pete and goes to put his arms around him and Pete is really uncomfortable because of the sexuality thing. The body language is so brilliant. Mike writes great embarassment.

'And the birth scene itself was very poignant for me, especially given the fact that we used twins to play the baby. But I love the scene. Fay Ripley understood obviously that this all meant something to me, so we played around with it a lot. Babies are always emotional anyway and Fay did a superb job. Because we were running out of time, the bulk of it was done in one take with a bit of ad-libbing – things like Rachel bursting into the room, leaning over and saying, "Can I touch him?" It's very syrupy, but it feels very real because it was done in one take with the camera moving around, going out of focus and then back into focus. John and Jimmy were just great, sobbing their eyes out. There was a lovely moment with the three of them together – Pete, Jenny and Adam – three mates with the baby.'

Fay Ripley (Jenny):

'For the birth scene I had to have a prosthetic tummy, which cost £2,000 and was moulded onto my body. And because it was quite graphic, I also had to wear a pubic wig, which was very generously applied by Janet Horsfield, the make-up designer. The head of department and no one else had to do that! It was very hot in the hospital room where we were filming. There were 90 grown men with ladders in there and me with my legs apart. I didn't have to act much in the end because I was absolutely exhausted, sweating like a pig with all this stuff on me. The only thing I really had to imagine was the pain. Then they produced this brand new, perfect little baby and attached an umbilical cord. The baby was so little. It was actually two weeks old, but had been born two weeks premature so it was authentic as a new-born baby. And my natural instincts were to look after this tiny baby. Normally at the end of a scene I'd be demanding coffee or whatever, but instead I was feeling very maternal towards this baby that was lying on my tummy.'

The Scripts

```
SCENE   63 INT
SET   TRAM
DAY 9   1132

ADAM:

AS BEFORE.              ┌─────────────────────────┐
                        │ NB PHONE CALL – REFER    │
                        │ ALSO TO SCENES 60, 61 & 62 │
                        └─────────────────────────┘

                    ADAM:

    (INTO PHONE)  Hello?  Hello?  (BEAT, TO HIMSELF)  Oh

    shit!

ADAM PUNCHES OUT A PHONE NUMBER AND WAITS NERVOUSLY FOR IT
TO BE ANSWERED.

                    ADAM:

    Come on!  Come on!  (BEAT)  Pete?!
```

> NB PHONE CALL – REFER ALSO
> TO SCENE 64

CUT TO

SCENE 64 INT
SET PETE'S OFFICE
DAY 9 1132

SECRETARY:

A SECRETARY STANDS AT PETE'S DESK, SPEAKING ON HIS PHONE.

> NB PHONE CALL – REFER ALSO
> TO SCENE 63

SECRETARY:

(INTO PHONE) I'm afraid he's not at his desk at the

moment.

INTERCUT BETWEEN ADAM AND THE SECRETARY.

ADAM:

(FRANTICALLY) Well, where is he?!

THE SECRETARY PURSES HER LIPS, NOT LIKING THE CALLER'S RUDE
MANNER.

SECRETARY:

I don't know. I'm not his secretary.

ADAM:

Well, where's *she*?!

SECRETARY:

Off sick. I think he's got a mobile. You could try

him on that.

ADAM:

I'm on his mobile! Look, his wife's gone into labour.

We've got to find him!

SECRETARY:

Hang on, his diary's here. (A COUPLE OF BEATS) Uh oh.

ADAM:

"Uh oh"! What does that mean?

SECRETARY:

This morning's crossed out. And it doesn't say

why.

ADAM STARES HORROR-STRICKEN INTO THE MIDDLE DISTANCE, UNSURE OF WHAT TO DO NEXT.

CUT TO

SCENE 65 INT
SET   RACHEL'S OFFICE
DAY 9 1200

RACHEL:
ADAM:

RACHEL SITS AT HER DESK IN HER OWN CUBICLE, SPEAKING ON THE PHONE AS ADAM APPEARS, PANTING HEAVILY. HE'S TOO OUT OF BREATH TO SPEAK. TO GET RACHEL'S ATTENTION, HE PRESSES HIS HAND DOWN ON THE PHONE CUTTING OFF THE CALL.

RACHEL:

Adam! What do you think you're doing?! I was talking

to Karen. (REMEMBERS) And I'm not talking to you!

ADAM:

(GASPING) Jenny! Into labour!

RACHEL:

What?

ADAM:

Can't find Pete.

RACHEL:

Well, call him on his mobile?

ADAM BRINGS HIS HAND OUT FROM BEHIND THE PARTITION TO REVEAL THE MOBILE IN QUESTION.

RACHEL:

Oh shit.

ADAM:

Please help me find him.

RACHEL NODS. CURRENT HOSTILITIES ARE SUSPENDED IN THE FACE OF THIS LARGER CRISES.

RACHEL:

Where do you think he'll be.

ADAM:

(HANDING HER A PIECE OF PAPER) I've drawn up a list of

possible places.

RACHEL:

(CONSULTING THE LIST) Most of these are pubs. Plus a

gym.

ADAM:

Start with the pubs. I'm going to the hospital.

HE DASHES OUT. RACHEL GRABS HER COAT OFF THE BACK OF HER
CHAIR AND HURRIES AFTER HIM.

CUT TO

SCENE 66 INT
SET TAXI
DAY 9 1210

ADAM:
CABBIE:

ADAM SITS NERVOUSLY IN THE BACK OF A BLACK CAB WHICH
MEANDERS ITS WAY THROUGH THE CITY CENTRE STREETS.

ADAM:

Can you maybe step on it a bit? I'm on my way to a

birth.

CABBIE:

(SPEEDING UP) Oh, right! Your wife, is it?

ADAM:

No, we're not married. Well, she is. To my best mate.

CABBIE:

(NOT SURE WHAT TO MAKE OF THIS) Right.

CUT TO

SCENE 67 EXT
SET TWO ADJOINING PUBS
DAY 9 1220

RACHEL:

RACHEL'S MINI CAREERS TO A HALT (ITS FRONT WHEELS
HAPHAZARDLY ON THE PAVEMENT) OUTSIDE TWO ADJOINING PUBS.
RACHEL LEAPS OUT AND SPRINTS INTO THE LEFT HAND PUB. THE
CAMERA PANS OVER TO THE RIGHT IN TIME TO SEE RACHEL DASHING
OUT OF THE *SECOND* PUB. SHE SPRINTS BACK TOWARDS HER CAR.

CUT TO

SCENE   68 INT
SET   TAXI
DAY 9   1221

ADAM:
CABBIE:

THE CAB SITS IN A LINE OF TRAFFIC. ADAM HOPS ABOUT
NERVOUSLY IN THE BACK.

ADAM:

What's the hold up?

CABBIE:

(PEERING AHEAD) Looks like a burst water main. (HE

SWINGS THE CAB ROUND IN THE ROAD) It's alright. I

know a back way. So, your best mate, whose wife

is giving birth. Is he going to be there?

ADAM:

He doesn't know about it. Why do you think I'm going?

FROM THE DISGUSTED LOOK THE CABBIE GIVES ADAM IN HIS REAR
VIEW MIRRO (UNSEE BY ADAM), IT'S BECAUSE HE THINKS ADAM IS
THE FATHER.

CUT TO

SCENE   69 INT
SET   WINEBAR
DAY 9   1230

RACHEL:
KAREN:

KAREN SITS ALONE AT A SMALL TABLE IN A TRENDY WINEBAR,
NURSING A GLASS OF WHITE WINE AND PERUSING THE MENU, AS
RACHEL DASHES IN.

RACHEL:

(FRANTICALLY) Karen, I can't stop for lunch. Jenny's

gone into labour and Pete's gone missing!

KAREN:

(CALMLY) He's playing golf with David.

THIS NEWS STOPS RACHEL DEAD IN HER TRACKS. MOMENTARILY.

RACHEL:

Come on!

SHE RUSHES OUT. KAREN FUMBLES A FIVER ONTO THE TABLE AND
HURRIES AFTER HER.

CUT TO

SCENE 70 EXT
SET GOLF COURSE
DAY 9 1231

DAVID:
PETE:

DAVID (IN ALL THE RIGHT GOLF GEAR) AND PETE (IN WHATEVER
WOULD PASS MUSTER) ARE ON A GREEN. PETE IS PUTTING, 'AIDED'
BY DAVID, WHO'S STANDING RIGHT UP AGAINST HIM - GROIN TO
ARSE. DAVID HAS HIS ARMS ROUND PETE, HOLDING PETE'S ARMS AS
HE TAKES A SWING. (PETE LOOKS DEEPLY UNCOMFORTABLE.) THE
BALL DRIBBLES FOUR FEET AND INTO THE HOLE.

                    DAVID:

    Jolly good! Call it ten, shall we? And I was a four.

DAVID, VERY PLEASED WITH HIMSELF, MARKS UP THE SCORECARD
(ONLY DAVID WOULD KEEP SCORE AGAINST A TOTAL NOVICE), THEN
STRIDES OFF CHEERFULLY TO THE NEXT GREEN. PETE, LOOKING LIKE
HE MIGHT KILL DAVID BEFORE THE ROUND IS OVER, BENDS DOWN TO
RETRIEVE HIS BALL.

CUT TO

SCENE 70A INT
SET RACHEL'S CAR
DAY 9 1231
                                **NEW SCENE ISSUED 09/03/98
RACHEL:
KAREN:

RACHEL AND KAREN RACE ALONG IN RACHEL'S CAR, ON THEIR WAY TO
THE GOLF COURSE. THEY'RE BOTH TENSE, THEIR CONVERSATION
REDUCED TO THE BARE ESSENTIALS.

                    KAREN:

    A to Z?

                    RACHEL:

    Glove compartment.

KAREN TRIES TO OPEN THE GLOVE COMPARTMENT; SHE CAN'T.

                    KAREN:

    Locked.

                    RACHEL:

    Hit it.

KAREN HITS IT. IT SPRINGS OPEN. SHE FISHES AROUND INSIDE.

RACHEL:

Found it?

KAREN:

(TAKING STUFF OUT OF GLOVE COMPARTMENT) Hmmm... Sweet

wrappers.... gloves.... *more* sweet wrappers?...

RACHEL:

Adam's.

KAREN:

(TRIUMPHANTLY PRODUCES A TO Z) A to Z!

THE DISCOVERY OF THE A TO Z MEANS THEY CAN RELAX A LITTLE.
KAREN STARTS LOOKING FOR THE GOLF COURSE.

RACHEL:

Does this remind you of when you gave birth?

KAREN:

Racing to a golf course? Actually, I don't remember

that much. Drugged up to the eyeballs.

RACHEL:

David was there, wasn't he?

KAREN:

(NODS) Even cancelled a meeting.

RACHEL:

Well, it was his first-born... We just turned on to

the B243.

KAREN LOOKS AT A SIGN-POST AS THEY FLASH PAST IT, THEN BACK
AT HER A TO Z.

KAREN:

O-kayyy. Right road. Wrong direction.

RACHEL LOOKS AT HER, HORRIFIED. KAREN OFFERS HER A SICKLY
SMILE - UNFORTUNATELY IT'S TRUE. RACHEL JUMPS ON THE
BRAKES, DOING AN EMERGENCY STOP.

CUT TO

SCENE 71 EXT
SET HOSPITAL
DAY 9 1232

ADAM:
CABBIE:

THE CAB PULLS UP. ADAM LEAPS OUT AND THRUSTS A £20 NOTE
THROUGH THE CABBIES WINDOW.

> CABBIE:
>
> (FULL OF HOSTILITY) Keep your money! I hope it chokes
>
> you.

THE CAB DRIVES OFF. ADAM IS LEFT MOMENTARILY WONDERING WHAT
THE CABBIE'S PROBLEM WAS, THEN DISMISSING THIS THOUGHT,
RACES TOWARDS THE HOSPITAL ENTRANCE.

CUT TO

SCENE 72 EXT
SET GOLF COURSE
DAY 9 1240

DAVID:
PETE:
RACHEL:
KAREN: **AMENDED 18/02/98

DAVID STANDS HOLDING THE FLAG AS PETE TAKES A SIX FOOT PUTT.
IT MISSES AND RUNS ABOUT SIX FEET PAST THE HOLE. PETE
SWEARS TO HIMSELF.

> DAVID:
>
> Hard luck.

PETE CROSSES TO THE OTHER SIDE AND IS AGAIN ADDRESSING THE
BALL WHEN HE AND DAVID *ARE DISTRACTED BY A COMMOTION IN THE
DISTANCE. THEY LOOK UP TO SEE A CAR RACING ACROSS THE
COURSE, ITS HORN BLARING; OTHER GOLFERS SCATTER. DAVID AND
PETE STARE IN AMAZEMENT.

> PETE:
>
> *Rachel's got a car like that.
>
> DAVID:
>
> *(PEERING AT APPROACHING CAR) That is Rachel. And
>
> Karen.
>
> PETE:
>
> *Must be some kind of drama. (SUDDENLY REALISES WHAT'S
>
> THE MOST LIKELY CAUSE) Oh my God!!

PETE THROWS HIS PUTTER ASIDE AND SPRINTS OFF TOWARDS THE
*APPROACHING CAR.

DAVID:

(CALLING AFTER PETE) You haven't putted out!

CUT TO

SCENE 73 INT
SET HOSPITAL - OUTSIDE/INSIDE DELIVERY ROOM
DAY 9 1241

ADAM:
JENNY:
MIDWIFE:

ADAM ARRIVES OUTSIDE A ROOM WHICH BEARS THE SIGN "DELIVERY
ROOM 3". HE DITHERS NERVOUSLY, UNSURE OF WHETHER TO GO IN
OR NOT. HE ALMOST KNOCKS THEN ISN'T SURE IF THIS IS CORRECT
FORM. HIS DITHERING IS INTERRUPTED BY THE EMERGENCE FROM
THE ROOM OF AN EFFICIENT AND MATRONLY MIDDLE-AGED MIDWIFE.

MIDWIFE:

Have you come for Jenny Gifford?

ADAM:

Yes. Has she had it yet?

MIDWIFE:

No, don't worry, you're still in time. In you go!

ADAM:

No, I'll just... (wait out here)

AMENDED 18/02/98

IGNORING ADAM'S PROTESTATION, THE MIDWIFE HUSTLES HIM INTO
THE DELIVERY ROOM. *SHE GOES TO GET SOMETHING FROM THE
TABLE.* HE'S MET BY THE SIGHT OF JENNY, FLAT OUT ON A BED,
HER LEGS AKIMBO IN THE BIRTHING POSITION. HER FACE COVERED
BY A GAS MASK, SHE DOESN'T SEE HIM. A CONTRACTION FORCES
HER TO LEAP UP WITH A SCREAM OF AGONY. ADAM LOOKS UTTERLY
HORRIFIED AT WHAT HE'S STUMBLED INTO.

CUT TO

SCENE 74 INT
SET RACHEL'S CAR
DAY 9 1250

REWRITTEN 09/03/98

RACHEL:
PETE:

RACHEL AND PETE HARE BACK TO MANCHESTER IN HER MINI. BOTH
ARE IN A STATE OF ADVANCED NERVOUS EXCITEMENT. *PETE IS
FRANTICALLY TRYING TO FIND THE RIGHT PAGE IN THE A TO Z.*

PETE:

*(MUTTERING) I should never have let him borrow my

mobile.

RACHEL:

*(LOOKING OVER AT HIM; URGENTLY) Have you found it yet?

PETE:

*(SHAKING THE A TO Z IN FRUSTRATION) My maps are a

different scale! Maybe we should go home for them.

RACHEL:

*No! Keep looking! You can't lose a hospital.

*PETE RESUMES TURNING THE PAGES OF THE A TO Z. HE TAKES A
DEEP BREATH.

PETE:

*(ALMOST TO HIMSELF; MANTRA-LIKE) Okay, Jen, I'll be

there. Don't worry. Baby, Daddy's on is way. Just

hold on.

*RACHEL SNEAKS A LOOK ACROSS AT PETE, AND SMILES
AFFECTIONATELY. HE DOESN'T SEE, HIS HEAD IS BURIED IN THE A
TO Z.

PETE:

*(TRIUMPHANTLY) Okay! Got it!

RACHEL:

*The hospital?

**REWRITTEN 09/03/98

PETE:

*(IN ALL SERIOUSNESS) No, Old Trafford. But it's

close.

RACHEL:

*So, which way?

PETE:

*What time is it?

RACHEL:

*What?

PETE:

*(CONSULTING HIS WATCH) Almost one. That would make

it... the blue route.

*RACHEL HAS NO IDEA WHAT HE'S ON ABOUT.

RACHEL:

*A simple left or right would do.

PETE:

*Next right, then left, over the roundabout, second

right, left, left, then right.

RACHEL:

*So that was next... left?

PETE:

*Right! (FRANTICALLY) *As in right!!*

CUT TO

SCENE 75 INT
SET HOSPITAL - DELIVERY ROOM
DAY 9 1251

ADAM:
JENNY:
MIDWIFE:

ADAM STILL STANDS NERVOUSLY OUT OF THE WAY BY THE DOOR AS
THE MIDWIFE RE-ENTERS THE DELIVERY ROOM. JENNY IS AS YET
UNAWARE OF HIS PRESENCE.

MIDWIFE:

(TO ADAM) Come on, don't be shy! Birthing partners

are allowed at the bedside.

SHE PUSHES HIM FORWARD TOWARDS JENNY, WHO REMOVES HER GAS
MASK AND LOOKS AT HIM.

JENNY:

Pete, thank God you're... Adam!

ADAM:

Hi, Jen. How's it going?

MIDWIFE:

(TO JENNY) This isn't your husband?

ADAM:

He's on his way. Possibly. (TO JENNY) Look, I can

wait outside if you'd prefer.

ANOTHER CONTRACTION STARTS TO CONSUME JENNY. SHE GRABS
ADAM'S HAND AND AS THE CONTRACTION HITS, DIGS HER NAILS IN.
HIS FACE CONTORTS IN AGONY, HIS MOUTH OPENING IN A SILENT
SCREAM, THE SOUND FOR WHICH IS PROVIDED BY JENNY.

CUT TO

<u>SCENE 76 EXT</u>
<u>SET MANCHESTER CITY STREET</u>
<u>DAY 9 1252</u>

RACHEL:
PETE:
MOTORCYCLE COP:
Cop 2 n/s:

RACHEL'S CAR ZIPS THROUGH THE CENTRE OF MANCHESTER.

PETE:

(TRYING TO REMEMBER) This time of day, the blue

route... Next left!

WITH A SCREECH OF TYRES, RACHEL SWINGS THE CAR TO THE
LEFT... THE WRONG WAY DOWN A ONE WAY STREET. COMING IN THE
OPPOSITE DIRECTION ARE TWO POLICEMEN RIDING MOTORCYCLES.

PETE:

Or maybe it was next but one.

RACHEL'S CAR SCREECHES TO A HALT, INCHES AWAY FROM THE
ONCOMING MOTORBIKE COPS. PETE LEAPS OUT OF THE CAR AND RUNS
TOWARDS THE DISMOUNTING COPS. RACHEL FOLLOWS.

PETE:

Officers, this is an emergency!

MOTORCYCLE COP:

(TAKING OUT NOTEPAD - UNIMPRESSED) Of course it is,

sir.

PETE:

It's my wife! She's giving birth. And I'm going to

miss it!

THE POLICEMAN STOPS WRITING DOWN RACHEL'S REGISTRATION
NUMBER AND LOOKS AT HER.

MOTORCYCLE COP:

Is this true?

RACHEL NODS URGENTLY. THE COP LOOKS AT PETE, (WHO'S BESIDE
HIMSELF WITH ANXIETY).

MOTORCYCLE COP:

Every father should see his child being born. (TO HIS

COLLEAGUE) Matthews, your helmet!

CUT TO

SCENE 77 INT
SET HOSPITAL - DELIVERY ROOM
DAY 9 1253

JENNY:
ADAM:
MIDWIFE:

JENNY'S BIRTH IS APPROACHING. SHE'S SWEATING AND PANTING.
ADAM STANDS AT HER HEAD, STARING AT HIS WATCH. THE MIDWIFE
STANDS AT THE BUSINESS END, INSPECTING THE CERVIX.

JENNY:

(TO MIDWIFE) What stage am I at?

ADAM:

(PRESUMING THIS COMMENT'S DIRECTED AT HIM) Well, I'm

no expert, but I'd definitely say it was labour.

ANOTHER CONTRACTION SWEEPS ACROSS JENNY. ADAM PRESSES A
BUTTON ON HIS WATCH, WHICH BEEPS.

ADAM:

(CONSULTING HIS WATCH) Two minutes **twenty three** point

two! They're getting closer!

MIDWIFE: ****AMENDED 18/02/98**

(TO JENNY) You're fully dilated now, **Jenny.**

JENNY PUSHES ADAM IN THE DIRECTION OF THE END OF THE BED.

JENNY:

(TO ADAM, PANTING) Tell me what you can see!

ADAM TRIES TO STAY WHERE HE IS.

ADAM:

No, really, the view from here's just fine.

JENNY:

(SCREAMING AT HIM) Get down the bed, you

*tossssaaaaaghhhh!!! *AMENDED 18/02/98

SHE HOWLS AS SHE PUSHES. ADAM KNOWS WHEN TO DO AS HE'S TOLD
AND SCURRIES DOWN THE BED. HE STANDS STARING AT JENNY'S
MOST INTIMATE PARTS, ATTEMPTING A REASSURING SMILE, BUT
FAILING TO MASK AN EXPRESSION OF COMBINED FASCINATION AND
HORROR.

CUT TO

SCENE   78 EXT
SET   MANCHESTER STREET
DAY 9   1255

PETE:
MOTORCYCLE COP:

THE BIKE, WITH PETE AND THE MOTORCYCLE COP ABOARD, WEAVES
ITS WAY AT HIGH SPEED THROUGH TRAFFIC, LIGHTS FLASHING AND
SIREN BLAZING.

CUT TO

SCENE   79 INT
SET   HOSPITAL - DELIVERY ROOM
DAY 9   1258

ADAM:
JENNY:
MIDWIFE:

ADAM IS TRYING NOT TO LOOK AT JENNY'S VAGINA, MUCH IN THE
WAY ONE LOOKS SLIGHTLY OFF TO ONE SIDE OF A CINEMA SCREEN
DURING THE WORST BITS OF A SLASHER MOVIE. HE DARES TO DRAG
TO HIS EYES TO THE OFFENDING SPOT AND SUDDENLY HIS LOOK OF
HORROR GIVES WAY TO ONE OF EXCITEMENT.

                    ADAM:

    Oh, Jenny! Jenny! I can see its head!

                    **AMENDED 18/02/98

*JENNY STARTS TO PUSH.

                    MIDWIFE:

    *Now Jenny, don't push. Remember your breathing.

*JENNY, ADAM AND THE MIDWIFE ALL BREATH TOGETHER.

CUT TO

SCENE 80 EXT
SET   HOSPITAL
DAY 9 1320

PETE:
MOTORCYCLE COP:

THE POLICE MOTORBIKE SCREECHES TO A HALT OUTSIDE THE
HOSPITAL ENTRANCE. PETE LEAPS OFF THE BACK AND RACES
TOWARDS THE ENTRANCE, THE CRASH HELMET STILL ON HIS HEAD.

CUT TO

SCENE 81 INT
SET HOSPITAL - DELIVERY ROOM
DAY 9 1320

ADAM:
JENNY:
MIDWIFE:

ADAM IS HOLDING JENNY IN HIS ARMS, HIS EARLIER
SQUEAMISHNESS AND EMBARRASSMENT IS COMPLETELY FORGOTTEN AS
ADAM IS CAUGHT UP IN THE WONDER OF CHILDBIRTH. THE PERFECT
BIRTHING PARTNER, HE'S HARANGUING JENNY LIKE A FOOTBALL
COACH.
                              **AMENDED 18/02/98
                    ADAM:

Come on, Jenny! * Come on.

                    MIDWIFE:

*The baby's head is nearly born, Jenny. Push!

                    JENNY:

(SOBBING WITH PAIN AND EXHAUSTION) I'm too tired. I

can't.

                    ADAM:

(VEHEMENTLY) Yes you can, girl! You've got the

strength! Now come on! Push!!!

                    MIDWIFE:

*Let your body do the work. You can do it. You're

doing really well. The baby's nearly here.

CUT TO

SCENE 82 INT
SET HOSPITAL - CORRIDOR
DAY 9 1323

PETE:
Patient n/s:
Porter n/s:

PETE, STILL WEARING HIS HELMET, RACES DOWN A
CORRIDOR. SUDDENLY, AS IF FROM NOWHERE (BUT FROM A SIDE
PASSAGE) A TROLLEY BEARING A PATIENT APPEARS IN HIS PATH.
WITHOUT BREAKING HIS STRIDE, PETE HURDLES THE TROLLEY AND
LANDS THE OTHER SIDE, CONTINUING TO SPRINT ALONG THE
CORRIDOR, (HE DOESN'T LOOK BACK). THE PATIENT ON THE
TROLLEY SITS UP AND STARES IN ASTONISHMENT AFTER PETE'S
RETREATING BACK, AS DOES THE PORTER.

CUT TO

SCENE 83 INT
SET HOSPITAL - CORRIDOR
DAY 9 1323

PETE:

A PEACEFUL CORRIDOR. DOCTORS AND PATIENTS GO ABOUT THEIR
BUSINESS. FROM AN UNSEEN SIDE CORRIDOR PETE SUDDENLY SKIDS
INTO VIEW, UNABLE TO STOP ON THE POINTED STUDS OF HIS GOLF
SHOES. HE SLIDES ACROSS THE CORRIDOR AND OUT OF VIEW, HIS
HANDS GRABBING THE CORRIDOR WALL TO STOP HIM. HIS FEET
FINALLY GETTING TO GRIP, PETE MANAGES TO DRAG HIMSELF INTO
THE CORRIDOR. HE SPRINTS UP IT, OTHER PEOPLE TACTFULLY
GIVING WAY.

CUT TO

SCENE 84 INT
SET HOSPITAL - DELIVERY ROOM
DAY 9 1324

ADAM:
JENNY:
MIDWIFE:
PETE:
RACHEL:
MOTORCYCLE COP:
Cop 2 n/s:

AS BEFORE. THE MIDWIFE IS NOW HANDS ON. JENNY MOANS AND
GRUNTS AND PANTS AS SHE CLINGS TO ADAM.

                    ADAM:

    Come on, Jen! Fantastic! You're almost there.

SPURRED ON BY ADAM'S ENCOURAGEMENT, JENNY GIVES ANOTHER
MIGHTY HEAVE, THEN FALLS BACK ONTO THE SHEETS.

                    ADAM:

    Just one more push should do it!

                    JENNY: **AMENDED 18/02/98

    *Shut up!

JENNY PANTS THEN GOES FOR IT BIG-TIME.

                    JENNY:

    Gnnnnnnnnnnnnnnnnnnnnr!

MID PUSH, THE DOORS TO THE DELIVERY ROOM FLY OPEN AND PETE
CRASHES INTO THE ROOM CLUTCHING HIS HELMET, SKIDDING ACROSS
THE FLOOR TO ARRIVE AT ADAM'S SIDE.

                    PETE:

    Jenny! Darling! I'm here!

JENNY COLLAPSES BACK ONTO THE BED, THE MIDWIFE REACHES IN
AND A BABY'S CRY IS HEARD.

                    MIDWIFE:

    And so is the baby!

PETE AND ADAM LOOK STUNNED AT ONE ANOTHER, THEN BOTH BURST
INTO TEARS AND FALL INTO EACH OTHER'S ARMS. THE MIDWIFE
CARRIES THE BABY TO PLACE IT ON JENNY'S CHEST. PETE,
SOBBING, GOES TO CUDDLE JENNY, BOTH AD-LIBBING ENDEARMENTS.
("HE'S GOT YOUR NOSE", "HE'S PERFECT" ETC) ADAM, QUITE
OVERWHELMED, JOINS IN PETE AND JENNY'S CUDDLE,

**AMENDED 18/02/98

JENNY:

(TO PETE) We haven't got a boy's name.

PETE LOOKS UP TO SEE THE MOTORCYCLE COP WHO'S QUIETLY
ENTERED THE ROOM

PETE:

Officer, what's your name?

MOTORCYCLE COP:

Preston, sir.

PETE:

I meant your first name.

MOTORCYCLE COP:

That is my first name.

PETE:

(FLATLY) Oh.

JENNY:

(LOOKING FONDLY AT ADAM) We'll call him Adam.

PETE:

Adam Preston Gifford.

ADAM, WHO'S ONLY JUST GOT HIS CRYING UNDER CONTROL, BREAKS
UP AGAIN. RACHEL AND THE SECOND MOTORCYCLE COP BURST INTO
THE DELIVERY ROOM. ADAM FALLS INTO RACHEL'S ARMS, SOBBING
HEAVILY.

Director Declan Lowney:

'At the end of episode one after the baby scene, Adam and Pete were drunk and Mike wrote a scene where they were playing crazy golf in the corridor. We shot that, but I didn't really like it much so at the end of my block of 12 days' filming, I rushed like mad one day to get finished early. I had half an hour left and I put Jimmy and John together and said: "Look, you're drunk, it's the middle of the night, talk. Talk about how much you admire Jenny giving birth to that kid." And we turned over. John put his head down, acting as if he was asleep, and Jimmy just talked ... "I was with her, I saw this, I saw everything. You know, Pete, I love her, I just think she's great." All that stuff. And Pete's just going "Uh?" I just told them what to talk about and they improvised the rest. No script, nothing. We just did it in one take. And that little 30-second scene turned out to be pertinent to what happens between Adam and Jenny later. I think Mike or Christine saw that scene and realized there was a basis for a future attraction between Adam and Jenny.'

Publicist Ian Johnson:

'I love the fantasy scene in the bar, where Jenny talks to Rachel and Karen about being a poor, defenceless Victorian chambermaid, taken by the firm but fair hand of her master. Fay Ripley wrote some of that scene herself and the way it ends – with Jenny muttering into her glass of wine "something like that" – always makes me cry with laughter. Especially when the camera pans back to reveal Rachel and Karen looking quite stunned at Jenny's revelations.'

Fay Ripley (Jenny):

'Mike Bullen had written a fantasy about a Sumo wrestler, but we ended up with a Victorian maid. I hasten to add that the squire was not from my own personal fantasy, but I did use my imagination and didn't have to try too hard. I did wonder at the time whether it was likely, whether people do sit around, talking about their sexual fantasies. But then a few of the crew chipped in to say that it was similar to their own fantasy ... except theirs were slightly more x-rated.

'My red wine on set is nothing stronger than Ribena. As we're in Manchester, they tried me with Vimto, but I couldn't be doing with that. So I asked for Ribena because I'm a Southerner, really.'

Cold Feet – the best bits...

Director **Mark Mylod**:

'A scene of which I am particularly fond is the one where Jenny and Pete are indulging in their sexual fantasies. Jenny is astride Pete, giving it everything as a Victorian maid being beaten by the squire, but it's doing nothing for Pete until he visualizes the barmaid that he fancies. Then he climbs on top and the scene ends with a shot of John Thomson's bottom sticking up in the air. To me, that was the perfect end shot for that scene.'

Fay Ripley (Jenny):

'The fantasy sex scene wasn't my favourite day. Why? You try having sex with John Thomson! Apart from anything else, his fantasy becomes this exquisite blonde model who's a size 6. So basically, Marilyn Monroe takes over from Fay Ripley as Jenny Gifford – it doesn't do much for the ego. And yes, we both had clothes on underneath – in fact, I wore steel trousers!'

John Thomson (Pete):

'Sex scenes are awkward. In what other job would you come home and say you've been shagging somebody – legimately? It's just odd. A lot of people think they must be great to do, but it's not. They say it'll be a closed set, but a closed set technically is still 20 guys hanging around. Fay had her bits covered up with tape and I wore boxers. It was all simulated, of course. I've done more sex scenes in series three, so I've become a bit of a veteran. Each time you do it, it gets easier. And the director's right about my bum – I've got a lovely arse!

'In the scene before, Jenny announces that she'll only let Pete have sex if he uses a condom. He hasn't got any, so he runs down the street in his pyjamas in the middle of the night to the nearest pub. We did that scene at Burnage – where Oasis come from. It was a bit embarassing, having to do about five takes with all these lorries going past, blowing their horns at me, but I gave it hell for leather.'

Cold Feet – the best bits...

Publicist Ian Johnson:

'I've worked on many different shows, but what makes *Cold Feet* unique is that normally cynical journalists and reviewers will quote back whole scenes to me when they talk about it. For me, episode three of series one was the point at which Cold Feet really took off. That episode was the second one to be entered for the Golden Rose of Montreux and I remember watching it in a room full of European TV journalists. It was then that I realized how peculiarly British some of the humour in the series is. The British contingent were helpless with laughter, especially when Fay rode John like a Derby winner, whipping him with a rose, but it was too racy for most Europeans. Because the British are perceived as being quite reserved I think they were puzzled that we could produce a comedy that was so near the knuckle.'

The Sex in a Shop Window Scene, Series One, Episode Three

Writer Mike Bullen:

'The scene where Rachel fulfils her fantasy of having sex in a shop window was inspired by a girl I once went out with. She had the initials LB – I'll say no more than that – and it was her fantasy, too. I hasten to add she never persuaded me to take part, but the idea rather intrigued me as to why anyone would want to do it. When David hears about it, he reacts as if he's got a nasty smell under his nose and says: "It's a bit public, isn't it?" And Adam replies: "I think that's the point." This scenario must have stuck in my mind for 15 years because at the time I had precisely the same attitude to the suggestion as David.'

Director Mark Mylod:

'The sex in the shop window scene was the most complex – and therefore just about the most satisfying – scene I had to shoot. Adam manages to get the keys to a city centre charity shop from a guy at work, who does shifts there at the weekend, and who even arranges for a double bed to be placed in the window. But then it all starts to go wrong. Firstly, he and Rachel find themselves locked in till morning and secondly, at the height of their lovemaking, a stolen car, pursued by a police vehicle, smashes through the shop window and pushes the bed, with Adam and Rachel still in it, right the way through the store.

'We found an empty shop in Manchester, just around the corner from Piccadilly Station, to use for the night and our design department dressed it up with the bed and other bits and pieces to make it look like a genuine charity shop. And of course we told the police what we were doing so they didn't think our joyrider was the real thing. In conjunction with our stunt co-ordinator, Nik Powell, I then storyboarded the scene so that everything was planned in advance down to the last detail. I broke the scene down into three sections and that was how we shot it. The first section showed the car approaching the shop; the second section had the car going through the window; and the third had the car continuing on through the shop.

'We had a stunt driver in the car and we used a small ramp to lift the car over the pavement and up through the shop window. And we used a second ramp to help propel the car through the shop. Obviously, the trickiest of the three sections was where the car goes through the window, and because we were using real glass, we had to do it in one take. I had five cameras trained on the window and special charges were detonated in the glass on impact to produce a spectacular shattering effect. For that particular shot, we replaced Jimmy and Helen in the bed with stunt doubles. It would have been too risky to leave the actors in, particularly since Helen was pregnant at the time.

'It was a real dusk till dawn shoot. We started at 8 pm and carried on until the light came up. It was great fun. And the one thing I remember the most vividly is going into the hotel bar at six o'clock in the morning with the crew and having a couple of pints while all the businessmen were having their breakfasts. That was a great feeling, relaxing after a long shoot. And we'd really earned those drinks that night.'

Publicist Ian Johnson:

'The shop we used was a former bed warehouse, which was ideal, but unfortunately, the street it was in turned out to be the hub of Manchester's night-life low-life. We started doing the scene at around 11 pm, just as the pubs were turning out. And whilst we'd managed to close the street to traffic, there was nothing we could do about pedestrians. There was a pub nearby, where it was 10p a pint on a Wednesday night ... and this was a Wednesday night. No sooner had we started than girls who bore a startling similarity to the Fat Slags from Viz were careering down the street, clinging on to each other. At one point there was a cat fight between an extremely well-endowed girl in a skin-tight polka dot dress and her friend, which took place right outside the huge plate glass shop window, where Jimmy and Helen were sitting in their underwear. Lads kept coming up to me, asking what was going on. To minimize the disturbance, we pretended that we were filming a bed commercial because this was at the height of Friends mania and there was Helen, who was appearing in Friends at the time, before their very eyes, wearing a negligée in bed with Jimmy.

'I remember Helen went shopping in Manchester with her mother once and said: "I've had sex in that shop window and I had to dress up as Cleopatra in that shop window!" That was in Habitat, where she played Cleopatra beckoning to Adam as he walked past the window.'

Helen Baxendale (Rachel):

'It's true – I do seem to have done something in most shop windows in Manchester! I also did a scene with Fay in Kendal's department store, where I was choosing sexy underwear to turn Adam on. I can't say the sex in the shop window scene did much for me. I was pregnant, and it was a long night in a bit of a dodgy area. The car coming through the window was quite exciting, but apart from that, I just had to have sex with Jimmy a lot ...'

James Nesbitt (Adam):

'Doing love scenes is always awkward because it's a bizarre thing to do for a job. But I must say that spending the day – or in this case, the night – in bed with Helen Baxendale is a definite bonus. I enjoy sex with Helen. In fact, sex with anyone's quite good – that's on and off the camera. Basically, I just enjoy sex!

'I can see why Adam is attractive to both men and women because he's urbane, witty, charming, handsome ... No, the truth is that he's not plastic or drop-dead gorgeous – because I'm not drop-dead gorgeous – and therefore, he's not threatening. He's a mix of vulnerability and idiocy. He can be quite caring and funny, but he's never patronizing or superior. You can't really dislike him – he's a decent fella.'

Cold Feet – the best bits...

59

SCENE 66 EXT
SET OXFAM SHOP - DOOR
NIGHT 12 2230

RACHEL:
ADAM:

RACHEL LOOKS NERVOUSLY UP AND DOWN THE STREET AS ADAM
FUMBLES WITH A SET OF KEYS IN THE LOCK OF AN OXFAM SHOP IN A
RELATIVELY QUIETISH SHOPPING STREET. THE SHOP IS ONE OF THE
BIGGER ONES IN THE OXFAM RANGE. HE UNLOCKS THE DOOR & LETS
THEM IN.

                    RACHEL:

    Where did you get the keys?

                    ADAM:

    Bloke at work. (THEY ENTER THE BUILDING) He does shifts

    here at the weekend.

CUT TO

SCENE 66A INT
SET OXFAM SHOP
NIGHT 12 2230

ADAM:
RACHEL:

ADAM LEADS THE WAY INTO THE BODY OF THE OXFAM SHOP. A LIGHT
SHINES FROM A BACK ROOM.

                    RACHEL:

    Did you have to explain why you needed them?

                    ADAM:

    Just said we wanted to do some late night shopping.

    Course I had to explain!

RACHEL WINCES.

                    ADAM:

    Don't worry. He's cool. Even said he'd rearrange the

    shop for us.

AS ADAM SAYS THIS, HE STEPS INTO THE BODY OF THE SHOP AND
LOOKS IN THE WINDOW. SPOTLIGHTS SHINE ON A DOUBLE BED, ITS
COVERS (EXOTIC INDIAN FABRICS) PULLED INVITINGLY BACK.
OVERHEAD ONE OF THOSE GAUDY GLITTER BALLS TURNS REFLECTING
SPARKLY LIGHT AROUND THE WINDOW. ON EITHER SIDE OF THE BED
STAND GARDEN STATUES OF ADAM AND EVE. RACHEL LOOKS
DISCONCERTEDLY AT ADAM.

RACHEL:

(RELUCTANTLY)   Are you sure you want to do this?

ADAM:

Hey, what makes you happy makes me happy.

RACHEL NODS DISCONSOLATELY.   SHE WAS AFRAID OF THAT.

CUT TO

SCENE 68 INT
SET OXFAM SHOP
NIGHT 12 2240

ADAM:
RACHEL:

ALL THE LIGHTS AROUND THE BED HAVE BEEN EXTINGUISHED, BUT A
LOW GLOW STILL PENETRATES FROM THE STREET.   ADAM'S CLOTHES
HANG FROM THE STATUE OF ADAM; RACHEL'S ARE NEATLY ARRANGED
ON HER SIDE OF THE BED.   ADAM AND RACHEL ARE BESIDE EACH
OTHER IN BED - ADAM SITS HALF UP; RACHEL HUNKERS DOWN, THE
COVERS PULLED TIGHTLY UP TO HER NECK.

RACHEL:

Are you sure no one can see us?

ADAM:

(INDICATING OUT THE SHOP WINDOW)   Rachel, there *is* no

one to see us.

AT WHICH POINT, SOMEONE WALKS PAST THE WINDOW.   ADAM AND
RACHEL SQUEAL AND DIVE UNDER THE COVERS.   A BEAT, THEN THEY
REAPPEAR.

RACHEL:

Let's make it a quickie, shall we?

THERE'S A NOISE AT THE REAR OF THE SHOP.

RACHEL:

(WHISPERS)   What's that?!

THE LIGHT AT THE BACK OF THE SHOP GOES OUT.

RACHEL:

(HISSES)   Burglars!

ADAM:

Who'd burgle an Oxfam shop?!

THE MAIN DOOR IS OPENED AND SHUT. A KEY IS HEARD TURNING IN THE LOCK.

ADAM:

Or lock up afterwards?

HE LEAPS OUT OF BED TO INVESTIGATE, THEN COMES PADDING BACK.

ADAM:

(NERVOUSLY) Erm, we seem to have a problem.

RACHEL:

Why, you've got the key haven't you?

ADAM:

I've got *a* key. (BEAT) It's been double locked.
Office upstairs must have been working late.

RACHEL:

We're locked *in*?!

ADAM:

(CLIMBING INTO BED) Only till morning. Look, don't
worry. We can hide. Then when someone comes in, make
like we're customers... (ADAM MOVES TOWARDS HER) Look,
come on. We're here now. We may as well make the most
of it.

RACHEL LOOKS DECIDEDLY DUBIOUS ABOUT THIS WHOLE ENTERPRISE.
CUT TO

SCENE 71 INT
SET OXFAM SHOP
NIGHT 12 2305

ADAM:
RACHEL:
MOTORCYCLE COP:

ADAM AND RACHEL ARE ROLLING ROUND IN THE BED IN THE MIDST OF SEXUAL PASSION, OBLIVIOUS TO WHETHER ANYONE IS WATCHING THEM OR NOT.

RACHEL:

Oh, Jesus! Adam, I love you! Don't stop, don't stop!

ADAM GRUNTS IN REPLY. AN OLD MAN PEERS THROUGH THE WINDOW, TRYING TO MAKE OUT WHAT THE MOVEMENT IS INSIDE. SUDDENLY, SOMETHING BEHIND THE OLD MAN CATCHES HIS ATTENTION. HE LOOKS OVER HIS SHOULDER. HORROR REGISTERS BRIEFLY ON HIS FACE, BEFORE HE LEAPS TO ONE SIDE... AND A SOUPED UP BOY RACER CAR SCREAMS PAST HIM AND THROUGH THE WINDOW OF THE OXFAM SHOP. GLASS CASCADES IN ALL DIRECTIONS AS THE CAR COMES TO REST AT THE SIDE OF THE BED. ADAM AND RACHEL SCREAM AND LEAP UP, PULLING THE COVERS AROUND THEM. TWO JOY-RIDING TEENAGERS LEAP OUT OF THE CAR. ONE SCAMPERS ACROSS THE BONNET, THEY BOTH RUN ACROSS THE BED, (REGISTERING ADAM AND RACHEL) BEFORE LEAPING THROUGH THE SHOP WINDOW AND RACING AWAY. POLICE SIRENS APPROACH, THEN A BLUE FLASHING LIGHT PLAYS INTO THE SHOP AS A POLICE MOTORCYCLE SCREECHES TO A HALT.

MOTORCYCLE COP:

(SHOUTING INTO SHOP) Okay, don't move! Put your hands on your head!

ADAM AND RACHEL DO AS THEY'RE TOLD, DROPPING THE COVERS AND REVEALING THEIR NAKEDNESS. THE POLICEMAN PLAYS A FLASHLIGHT ACROSS THEM.

MOTORCYCLE COP:

Um, maybe you'd better put them down again.

ADAM AND RACHEL GRAB THE COVERS BACK. THE MOTORCYCLIST SHINES HIS LIGHT ON ADAM'S FACE AS HE CLIMBS THROUGH THE SHATTERED WINDOW INTO THE SHOP.

MOTORCYCLE COP:

Hey, don't I know you?

ADAM:

I don't have a record. Yet.

MOTORCYCLE COP:

I was at the birth of your mate's baby. Adam, isn't it?

ADAM:

Preston!

MOTORCYCLE COP:

How's the little fella doing?

ADAM:

Oh fine, great.

RACHEL:

He's just started smiling.

MOTORCYCLE COP:

That's always a lovely moment.

PRESTON SITS ON THE EDGE OF ADAM AND RACHEL'S BED. HE LOOKS
AROUND THE SHOP.

MOTORCYCLE COP:

(REFERRING TO THEIR CURRENT SITUATION) So, you wanna

tell me about it?

ADAM AND RACHEL EXCHANGE NERVOUS GLANCES.

CUT TO

SCENE 73 INT
SET OXFAM SHOP
NIGHT 12 2315

ADAM:
RACHEL:
MOTORCYCLE COP:

THE MOTORCYCLE COP SITS ON THE END OF THE BED. ADAM AND
RACHEL ARE BOTH NOW SITTING, WRAPPED IN THE COVERS.

ADAM:

Rachel wanted to make love in public.

> RACHEL:

No I didn't.

> ADAM:

It's your sexual fantasy!

> RACHEL:

And it was you who insisted on acting it out.

> ADAM:

(TO THE POLICEMAN) We've been having problems in bed.

> RACHEL:

(TO THE POLICEMAN) He hasn't been happy.

> ADAM:

Yes I have! It's you who's been dissatisfied.

> RACHEL:

Since when?!

A BEAT.

> ADAM:

You mean you haven't?

> RACHEL:

And you haven't either?

THEY LOOK AT EACH OTHER, FOR THE FIRST TIME REALISING THE
DEPTH OF THEIR MISUNDERSTANDING.

> MOTORCYCLE COP:

It's good to talk.

CUT TO

Writer Mike Bullen:

'In what became known as the sex episode, when David is concerned that he's impotent, he decides to seek 'professional' help, not as Adam presumes from a therapist, but from a prostitute. Well, you would, wouldn't you? Well, all right, no, most men wouldn't, but this is a comedy drama we're talking about here! Anyway, David's visit to Trixie is perhaps my favourite scene among the 17 episodes I've now written. Usually you sit at your computer keyboard, think about the location and the point of the scene then struggle your way through line by line, but this scene just flowed. It helps when you can visualize the actor delivering the lines (which is why writing *Cold Feet* gets easier, even though thinking up the storylines gets harder); Robert does embarrassment so well I found myself cringing just at the thought of poor David (who is usually so in control of every situation he's in) finding himself completely out of his element and out of his depth. Even though the intent of his visit is to sleep with another woman, I think you can't help but feel for him.'

<u>SCENE 56 INT</u>
<u>SET TRIXIE'S APARTMENT</u>
<u>NIGHT 10 2105</u>

DAVID:
TRIXIE:

DAVID FOLLOWS TRIXIE INTO THE OPEN-PLAN APARTMENT.

              DAVID:

Sorry, I didn't mean to come early.

              TRIXIE:

(REFERRING TO HER PREVIOUS VISITOR) That's okay,

neither did he.

SHE LAUGHS AT HER JOKE. DAVID DOESN'T GET IT. HE LOOKS
RATHER HELPLESSLY AT HER.

              TRIXIE:

(SEEKING TO PUT DAVID AT HIS EASE) Trade joke. You

want a drink?

              DAVID:

(WEAKLY) Please. Beer?

TRIXIE GOES TO THE KITCHEN COUNTER AND RETURNS WITH A BEER
FOR DAVID.

              DAVID:

Nice place you've got here.

              TRIXIE:

Well, if you're gonna work from home, you've gotta make

it comfortable.

SHE HANDS DAVID A CAN OF BEER, WHICH HE OPENS. FREUD WOULD
BE PROUD OF IT - IT SPURTS EVERYWHERE. DAVID AND TRIXIE
WATCH THE SHOWER OF BEER DISSIPATE.

              TRIXIE:

This is your first time, right?

DAVID:

How did you know?

TRIXIE SHRUGS - A LUCKY GUESS. DAVID FISHES ABOUT IN HIS
WALLET AND PULLS OUT A £50 NOTE.

DAVID:

I imagine you'd like to be paid up front.

TRIXIE:

That much TV gets right. (MEANING HER FEE) Eighty.

EMBARRASSED, DAVID FUMBLES IN HIS POCKET FOR MORE. SHE
POCKETS THE MONEY THEN, TO DAVID'S DISCOMFORT, UNDOES HIS
TIE AND STARTS UNBUTTONING HIS SHIRT.

TRIXIE:

What's your name, sweetheart?

DAVID:

(THE BRIEFEST PAUSE BEFORE HE ANSWERS) Adam.

TRIXIE:

And your real name?

DAVID:

David.

DAVID FLINCHES IN ANNOYANCE WITH HIMSELF. HE HADN'T MEANT
TO REVEAL THAT.

TRIXIE:

Okay, Adam. We're gonna take this real easy...

HIS SHIRT NOW HANGING OPEN, SHE STARTS ON DAVID'S BELT.
DAVID EMITS AN INVOLUNTARY STRANGLED CRY, SOMETHING AKIN TO
A SQUEAK. SHE THEN REACHES FOR HIS FLY. HE GRABS HER HAND
TO STOP HER.

DAVID:

Maybe we could talk first.

TRIXIE:

Whatever you want, Adam. The meter's running.

SHE SITS ON THE EDGE OF THE BED AND MOTIONS FOR HIM TO SIT
BESIDE HER.

DAVID:

Call me David. (HE SITS) What's your name?

TRIXIE:

Trixie.

DAVID:

I mean your *real* name.

BEAT, SHE REGARDS HIM COOLLY.

TRIXIE:

Trixie.

DAVID:

Oh. Sorry. (TRYING TO MAKE UP FOR HIS INSULT) It

suits you. (REALISES THIS ONLY DIGS HIM IN DEEPER,

FLOUNDERING) I mean...

TRIXIE:

(INTERRUPTING) Why are you here, David?

DAVID:

Oh God! (BEAT, HE HANGS HIS HEAD IN SHAME) I'm

impotent.

TRIXIE RISES AND CROSSES TO THE KITCHEN COUNTER TO GET
HERSELF A CAN OF BEER.

TRIXIE:

(MATTER OF FACTLY) No you're not.

DAVID:

(LOOKING UP) I'm not?

TRIXIE:

You used to do it, right? And you'll be able to do it

again. It's just at the moment you can't stand and

deliver.

DAVID:

(HOPEFULLY) Do you really think so?

TRIXIE RETURNS WITH HER BEER AND SITS BESIDE HIM. SHE OPENS
THE CAN, WITHOUT INCIDENT.

TRIXIE:

Sweetie, it's practically common. I must have seen it

six times. Hell, impotence has earned me... (SHE TRAILS

OFF, UNABLE TO DO THE MATHS QUICKLY)

DAVID:

(WITHOUT HESITATION) Four hundred and eighty pounds.

TRIXIE:

You work with figures, right? Look, no disrespect but

you're all the same - stressed out in high powered

jobs. I've had them all - a judge, surgeon, management

consultant...

DAVID:

(INTERRUPTING, INTRIGUED) Who was that?!

TRIXIE:

Make that *two* management consultants.

DAVID LOOKS SHEEPISH - FOUND OUT AGAIN.

DAVID:

Since this thing began my work has suffered. I used to

be a power in the office. Now I have to queue for

coffee. I've got to get my manhood back! If I could

just shag once...

TRIXIE:

(SHAKING HER HEAD) 'Scuse the pun, David, but you're

coming at this all wrong. You need to get on top of

your job, *then* your wife.

DAVID:

Do you think so?

TRIXIE:

Honey, I know so. The judge I mentioned? After seeing
me, he sent two bank robbers down for life. Their
families weren't best pleased, but his secretary was.

A BEAT, DAVID PULLS OUT HIS WALLET. HE STANDS TO LEAVE.

DAVID:

Trixie, you're a wonder. I feel like a new man. (HE
FORCES A £50 NOTE INTO HER HAND) Take this. Please.
I can't thank you enough.

TRIXIE ACCEPTS THE MONEY.

TRIXIE:

(SMILING AT HIM) I love guys who can't get it up. You
tip big. And don't leave a mess.

DAVID SMILES AT TRIXIE, RATHER ATTRACTED TO THE FLIRTATIOUS
AND CONFIDENT WOMAN. IF HE WEREN'T HAPPILY MARRIED...

CUT TO

Director Mark Mylod:

'A scene which I think is beautifully performed is the one where Karen finds herself humiliated outside Alexander Welch's hotel room. Welch, played by Denis Lawson, is this Booker Prize-winning author, who insists on Karen editing his latest steamy novel. They flirt unashamedly with each other and Karen is really flattered because she thinks he fancies her. She even boasts about it to Rachel and Jenny, especially when he says he wants to dedicate the book to her. It looks as if she's ready to have an affair with him and the opportunity appears to present itself when they have to spend the night away together at a hotel after he has given a lecture. She goes up to his room and he pours her a glass of champagne, but her hopes are crushed when a younger model emerges from the bathroom. Karen quickly makes her excuses and leaves, utterly humilated. She realizes she has made a complete fool of herself and stands outside his door, repeating over and over again: "Oh, my God" and then "shit". I thought Hermione was excellent in that scene and that's why it's one of my favourites.'

The Scripts

```
ACT THREE

SCENE  32 INT
SET  HOTEL ROOM
NIGHT 7  2100

KAREN:

KAREN, DRESSED TO KILL IN AN EVENING DRESS, STARES INTO THE
MIRROR OF HER HOTEL ROOM IN LIVERPOOL, TRYING TO GET HER
BREATHING UNDER CONTROL.  THE MINI-BAR STANDS OPEN AT HER
SIDE.  KAREN HOLDS A MINIATURE OF WHISKY - SHE UNSCREWS THE
TOP AND DOWNS THE BOTTLE.  SHE TAKES A FINAL CHECK IN THE
MIRROR - SHE'S READY!

CUT TO
```

SCENE 33 INT
SET HOTEL ROOM - ALEC'S ROOM
NIGHT 7 2102

KAREN:
ALEC:
TRUDI:

ALEC WELCH, WEARING A DRESSING GOWN, OPENS HIS DOOR TO
KAREN, WHO'S CARRYING HER EVENING BAG OVER HER SHOULDER.

                    ALEC:

    Karen! I was just on my way to you.

KAREN TAKES IN HIS DRESSING GOWN AND SMILES BROADLY - HER
INSTINCTS HAD BEEN RIGHT. FROM BEHIND HER BACK SHE WHIPS OUT
A BOTTLE OF CHAMPAGNE AND TWO CHAMPAGNE FLUTES.

                    KAREN:

    Champagne?

                    ALEC:

    (SURPRISED) Oh! Erm... Well, why not?

WELCH STANDS BACK TO LET KAREN INTO HIS ROOM

                    KAREN:

    I thought we should celebrate. The reading went so

    well!

                    ALEC:

    (PLEASED) It did rather, didn't it?

KAREN UNCORKS THE CHAMPAGNE AND FILLS THE TWO CHAMPAGNE
FLUTES.

                    ALEC:

    I was a little worried at first. The audience took

    some warming up.

                    KAREN:

    ("OH, RUBBISH!") They were putty in your hands.

ALEC:

(FLATTERED) The secret is to find someone to focus on.

Then give them all you've got.

KAREN:

(THINKING HE MEANS HER) And did you find someone to

focus on?

ALEC:

(WITH A HALF SMILE) I did as a matter of fact.

KAREN SMILES AT HIM MEANINGFULLY. STILL HOLDING THE BOTTLE,
SHE PICKS UP A (FILLED) CHAMPAGNE FLUTE AND RAISES IT TO HIM
IN A TOAST. HE RAISES AN (EMPTY) HOTEL GLASS TO BE FILLED.
KAREN'S A BIT THROWN BY THIS, AS THERE'S A SECOND FILLED
FLUTE ON THE SIDE, BUT RATHER THAN MAKE AN ISSUE OF IT, SHE
FILLS THE GLASS. HE TOASTS HER.

ALEC:

To a successful evening.

KAREN:

That's only just begun.

THEY CHINK GLASSES AND DRINK. THE DOOR TO ALEC'S BATHROOM
OPENS AND A SEXY YOUNG WOMAN EMERGES, CLAD ONLY IN A TOWEL.
KAREN LOOKS AT HER IN SHOCK, THEN BACK AT ALEC.

KAREN:

Who's that?!

ALEC:

Trudi! (TO YOUNG WOMAN, HANDING HER THE SECOND

CHAMPAGNE FLUTE) It was Trudi, wasn't it?

TRUDI:

(HAPPILY; SHE'S AN AIRHEAD) That's right.

ALEC:

This is Karen, my editor.

TRUDI GAILY EXTENDS HER HAND FOR KAREN TO SHAKE.

TRUDI:

(CHEERFULLY, WITHOUT EMBARRASSMENT) Hello!

SPEECHLESS, KAREN SHAKES IT.

ALEC:

Trudi was in the front row. You must have noticed her.

KAREN:

(SADLY) I'm not as observant as you think.

KAREN IS HAVING TROUBLE TAKING ALL THIS IN.

KAREN:

Alec, you said you were just coming to my room.

ALEC TAKES KAREN BY THE ARM AND STEERS HER OUT OF THE
HEARING OF TRUDI.

ALEC:

Yesss... Bit difficult. I wondered if you might have

any condoms.

A BEAT; KAREN IS MORTIFIED.

KAREN:

No. No, I'm sorry.

ALEC:

(EMBARRASSED) No, *I'm* sorry. I, I haven't embarrassed

you, have I?

KAREN GIVES HIM A SAD SMILE. THANK GOD HE'LL NEVER KNOW JUST
HOW EMBARRASSED SHE IS.

KAREN:

(PUTS DOWN GLASS AND BACKS OUT) Look, I should be

going.

ALEC:

No! Stay! Finish your drink.

KAREN:

You two have it. I... don't really like champagne.

CUT TO

Executive producer Andy Harries:

'For me, John Thomson and Fay Ripley rooted the first series. It was in that series that their characters really came to work their way into the affections of the audience. There were some wonderful storylines for both of them – all the problems of their sex life after the baby. It was things like that which just hadn't been done on British TV before – not in a dramatic/comedic way. It's something we all know about – that women tend not to want to have sex after having a baby, and men want to have sex even more because they probably haven't been getting a lot of sex before the birth. So it's a classic time of tension, of frustration, of confusion and misunderstanding, and of fantasies. The way Adam and Pete talk in the pub is typical of a lot of men. All over the country, men share the problems over a pint. It's part of British life, something with which people can identify.

'Episode four of series one, where Pete loses his Dad, is a great episode because there's that classic father/son thing, which is hugely real to so many different people. They have a problem communicating, what with the father getting older and, in Pete's case, finding his feet, getting married, having a child ... and then suddenly, it's death. There's a terrible void, especially when, as happened to Pete, you are parted on a less than conciliatory note. You never get round to saying the things you want to say. And death is always sudden. You always think there will be time to say goodbye, to have the discussions you want to, but very rarely is one given that freedom. I lost my Dad a few years ago and that had a massive impact on me. So this was a storyline which I felt strongly that we should work in and it gave us a very moving episode.'

John Thomson (Pete):

'I was gutted that I lost my Dad because I love Sam Kelly (who played him) so much to work with. He's an institution – stuff like *Porridge*, *'Allo, 'Allo*. It was very difficult to play the scene where he had died. Fortunately, I haven't experienced the death of a close relative so I didn't have anything personal to draw on. In the end, I decided not to break down or anything. Instead, I just did nothing and it worked.'

Cold Feet – the best bits...

Helen Baxendale (Rachel):

'This is my favourite *Cold Feet* episode, the one with the scene in the church after Pete's Dad has died. That was so sad, so moving and so true to life.'

```
SCENE  49 INT
SET   CHURCH
DAY 10 1130

JENNY:
PETE:
BABY ADAM:
RACHEL:
ADAM:
KAREN:
DAVID:
SHEILA:
VICAR:
PETE'S GRAN:
```

ADAM, PETE AND JENNY (WHO CRADLES THE BABY) SIT IN THE FRONT
ROW OF THE CONGREGATION AS SHEILA READS POORLY FROM THE
BIBLE. BY THE LOOKS OF THE CONGREGATION SHE'S BEEN DOING
THIS FOR SOME TIME. SHE ENDS, AS DAVID ENTERS AND THE
JAPANESE PERSON CREEP UP THE AISLE. DAVID SHAKES THE
JAPANESE PERSON'S HAND THANKING THEM FOR THEIR HELP. SHEILA
RESUMES HER SEAT. ADAM SLIPS OUT TO LET HER IN.

                    VICAR:

     Now we're going to hear from Adam's Godfather, and

     namesake, Adam Williams.

ADAM MAKES HIS WAY TO THE FRONT OF THE CHURCH, AS DAVID
SLIPS IN BESIDE KAREN. THERE'S STILL A CERTAIN COOLNESS
BETWEEN THEM.

                    DAVID:

     (WHISPERING TO KAREN) Have I missed much?

                    KAREN:

     Just Jenny's sister reading from the Bible.

                    DAVID:

     Thank God for that.

SHEILA LEANS OVER AND ASKS JENNY IF SHE CAN HOLD THE BABY.
ADAM TAKES SOME NOTES OUT OF HIS POCKET AND PREPARES TO
ADDRESS THE CONGREGATION.

                    ADAM:

     When a baby is born, everyone else moves up a

     generation.

UNHAPPY IN SHEILA'S ARMS, BABY ADAM STARTS TO CRY.
```
```

ADAM:

Pete, who's a son, is now a father....

THE BABY STARTS BAWLING HIS LITTLE HEART OUT. ADAM STOPS,
THROWN OFF HIS STRIDE. JENNY LEANS OVER TO TAKE BABY ADAM
BACK FROM SHEILA. HE QUIETENS INSTANTLY. JENNY MOUTHS
"SORRY" AT ADAM.

ADAM:

Where was I? Oh yeah. Fathers and sons. I asked

Pete's Dad, Algy, what it had been like for him to

become a father.

PETE:

(TO HIMSELF) This should be good.

ADAM:

(UNWRAPPING A PIECE OF PAPER) He sent me this.

A MOBILE PHONE RINGS. ADAM LOOKS UP, AGAIN DISTRACTED, TO
SEE DAVID ANSWERING IT, HISSING "HAI!", THEN RUSHING UP THE
AISLE OUT OF THE CHURCH, INDICATING TO THE JAPANESE PERSON
THAT THEY SHOULD FOLLOW. THEY DO. ADAM, ANNOYED, RETURNS
TO THE PIECE OF PAPER.

ADAM:

(READING) "Inevitably, parents love their children

more than their children ever love them. A father looks

at his son and sees a part of himself."

PETE SNORTS.

ADAM:

"They say, be careful what you wish for."

SOMEONE'S WATCH BEEPS THE HOUR. ADAM CAN BARELY CONTAIN HIS
IRRITATION.

ADAM:

"My wish for my son was that he grow up independent of

mind and strong of will. That he has drives me mad. It

also fills me with pride."

PETE:

(ASIDE TO JENNY) Then why isn't the old bastard here?

ADAM:

"I know that Pete will be a good father. I've seen the way he looks at his son. With love. A love that only a father can recognise. And which I recognise because it's how I look at Pete."

ANOTHER MOBILE PHONE RINGS, INTERRUPTING ADAM'S FLOW. THIS IS JUST TOO MUCH FOR HIM.

ADAM:

Oh, for God's sake!!

THE PHONE IS PETE'S. HE FUMBLES TO ANSWER IT.

SHEILA:

(SHOUTING AT ADAM)   You shouldn't blaspheme in church!

ADAM:

(SHOUTING BACK)   And you shouldn't heckle!

JENNY IS AWARE THAT PETE IS ASHEN FACED AND IN A STATE OF SHOCK.

JENNY:

Pete! What is it?

ALL EYES TURN TO PETE. HE LOOKS FROM JENNY TO ADAM.

PETE:

My Dad. He's dead.

CUT TO

In Our Hearts Forever
ALGERNON EDWARD GIFFORD
12th May 1939 - 10th April 1998
Husband of Audrey Rose
Father of Peter Algernon
Grandfather of
Adam Preston Algernon

Writer Mike Bullen:

'When David and Karen go to marriage guidance in episode five, I did my research and went to a Relate office. And I noticed that there was a panic button for the counsellor to hit in order to send for help. I wanted to incorporate the triggering off of the alarm in the script and I wrote that David accidentally sets off the panic button by leaning back in his chair. But the director, Nigel Cole, said he didn't know how to shoot this convincingly and felt that he would be unable to explain it to the actors if they had a problem with it. It's important that the actors feel confident about what they're doing, and therefore the director must feel confident about it, too. I didn't want to lose this scene, so we spent hours and hours discussing it. In the end, Nigel suggested that David could press the panic button deliberately to end the session because he doesn't want counselling. It was perfect. That scene was a joy and it was the result of real collaboration, a real creative process where we were all feeding off each other. That's one of the things about *Cold Feet* – everyone who works on the show genuinely cares about it.'

Robert Bathurst (David):

'The marriage guidance scene is definitely one of my favourites. It was a difficult balancing act because it was high comedy, but it was important to hit the comedy subtly. As written at one stage, it had David holding a fire extinguisher above his head and screaming and shouting and yelling. I love playing David because he has human flaws and he is too much of a coward to do anything overtly. Everything he does is much subtler and leaves him room for escape – he would never do something like that which would leave him so exposed. So I was concerned about that and we got it changed. We also did a close-up of me chewing the carpet, which left me with burns on my face, but they didn't use it. The security people jumped on me and they had me with my nose pressed on this heavy, bristly, nylon carpet. When I saw the end result, I thought, "I went through all that and they didn't even show it." '

Hermione Norris
(Karen):

'I thought the marriage guidance scene was particularly true to life because it shows the sexes' different attitudes to counselling. David can't see the point of it all and thinks everything is fine, while Karen is desperately trying to communicate that actually it's not. Men do seem to be reluctant when it comes to things such as marriage guidance.

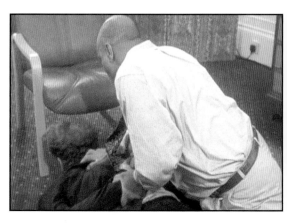

'Women quite like Karen because she's strong without being aggressive. In fact, I think she's a really lovely woman. She's sound – she's the strength behind the marriage. David thinks he wears the trousers and she is prepared to let him think that to an extent. So she manages to massage his ego and then does her own thing anyway.'

Cold Feet – the best bits...

SCENE 18 INT
SET MARRIAGE GUIDANCE OFFICE - WAITING ROOM
DAY 4 1900

KAREN:
DAVID:
COUNSELLOR:

KAREN SITS PATIENTLY IN THE WAITING ROOM OF A PLUSH
OFFICE, LEAFING THROUGH A MAGAZINE. THE DOOR TO THE
PASSAGEWAY IS OPEN. DAVID SUDDENLY APPEARS IN IT.

> KAREN:

(CHEERED) David! You've come!

> DAVID:

(WITHOUT ANY ENTHUSIASM; ENTERING) So it would appear.

(SITTING; COOLLY) You haven't begun without me, then?

> KAREN:

Should be a couple of minutes.

DAVID PICKS SOMETHING TO READ OFF THE TABLE. IT'S A BOOK
ABOUT MENDING RELATIONSHIPS. DAVID LOOKS AT THE TITLE,
SNIFFS, AND TOSSES IT IN A DESULTORY MANNER BACK ONTO THE
TABLE.

> DAVID:

Tell me, is our (DISTASTEFULLY) 'counsellor' a man or a

woman?

> KAREN:

Woman.

DAVID NODS - HE THOUGHT AS MUCH.

> DAVID:

The moment she uses the word 'facilitate' I'm out of

here.

SOMEWHERE OUT OF SIGHT A DOOR OPENS AND THE FOOTSTEPS OF A
COUPLE ARE HEARD, ALONG WITH SOBBING. KAREN LOOKS AT DAVID
AND RAISES HER EYEBROWS. THE COUPLE PASS THE OPEN DOOR OF
THE WAITING ROOM. DAVID AND KAREN STARE OUT AND SEE THAT
IT'S THE MAN WHO IS SOBBING, HIS PARTNER'S FACE STONY.
DAVID LOOKS HORRIFIED. BUT IT'S TOO LATE TO ESCAPE. THEIR
COUNSELLOR, A WOMAN IN HER LATE 50s, STICKS HER HEAD INTO
THE WAITING ROOM.

COUNSELLOR:

Mr and Mrs Marsden? Would you like to come this way?

THE COUNSELLOR DISAPPEARS. DAVID AND KAREN RISE, HIM AS
THOUGH PREPARING FOR BATTLE.

CUT TO

SET   MARRIAGE GUIDANCE OFFICE
DAY 4   1902

KAREN:
DAVID:
COUNSELLOR:
MALE COLLEAGUE:

THE COUNSELLOR USHERS DAVID AND KAREN INTO A COMFORTABLY,
APPOINTED OFFICE; EACH OF THEM CARRIES A CUP OF COFFEE. AT
THE ROOM'S CENTRE ARE THREE PADDED LEATHER CHAIRS ARRANGED
IN A TRIANGLE AROUND A COFFEE TABLE, ONE CHAIR AT THE APEX
FACING THE OTHER TWO WHICH ARE ALONGSIDE EACH OTHER. IN THE
BACKGROUND IS A DESK AND A CHAIR. A FIRE EXTINGUISHER
STANDS AGAINST ONE WALL. HANGING ON THE WALL, BEHIND THE
COUNSELLOR'S CHAIR IS A SMALL RED BUTTON, DISCREETLY MARKED
"ALARM".

COUNSELLOR:

I'm glad you were able to join us, Mr Marsden. Your

wife told me on the phone that you often have to work

late.

DAVID:

That hardly amounts to desertion.

THE COUNSELLOR AND KAREN ARE A LITTLE TAKEN ABACK, SINCE NO
ONE HAD SUGGESTED IT DID. THE COUNSELLOR MOTIONS TO THE
PADDED CHAIRS.

COUNSELLOR:

Please. Do sit down.

KAREN TAKES ONE OF THE TWO CHAIRS AT THE BASE OF THE
TRIANGLE; DAVID IMMEDIATELY SETTLES INTO THE CHAIR AT THE
APEX OF THE TRIANGLE, FACING HER.

COUNSELLOR:

(TO DAVID; EMBARRASSED) Um... that's my chair.

DAVID REALISES HIS MISTAKE. RATHER THAN GIVE GROUND, HE
LOOKS FOR ANOTHER REASON WHY HE SHOULD VACATE THE CHAIR. HE
STANDS AND PICKS UP HIS COFFEE FROM THE TABLE.

DAVID:

Perhaps I'll stand.

COUNSELLOR:

(INDICATING CHAIR ALONGSIDE KAREN) You might be more

comfortable sitting. (OFF DAVID'S COMBATIVE

EXPRESSION) Or maybe not.

THE COUNSELLOR LOOKS AT KAREN APOLOGETICALLY; KAREN SMILES
REASSURINGLY. THE COUNSELLOR SITS IN HER CHAIR.

COUNSELLOR:

Now, first, let me explain that my job is not to

prescribe, but to facilitate,...

DAVID EMITS A SMALL, STRANGLED CRY; KAREN SHOOTS HIM A
WARNING GLANCE.

COUNSELLOR:

...to enable you to understand any problems that you

might be having...

DAVID:

(INTERRUPTING) I've a question. (THE COUNSELLOR

REGARDS HIM) Are you married?

KAREN:

David!

DAVID:

(TO KAREN) It's a perfectly reasonable enquiry.

KAREN:

(TO COUNSELLOR) I'm terribly sorry.

DAVID:

(SLIGHTLY ACCUSING) It's just I noticed you're not

wearing a wedding ring.

A BEAT; THE COUNSELLOR DECIDES TO ANSWER THE QUESTION.

COUNSELLOR:

I'm a widow.

DAVID:

Oh.

COUNSELLOR:

But prior to my husband's death we were separated.

DAVID:

(LEAPING ON THIS) Ah ha! Then what makes you think

you're qualified for this job?

COUNSELLOR:

Thirty years experience?

DAVID:

(RELUCTANTLY) Yes, I suppose that would count for

something.

THE COUNSELLOR TAKES ADVANTAGE OF DAVID BEING THROWN
MOMENTARILY OFF-BALANCE TO PLUNGE AHEAD WITH THE
PRELIMINARIES.

COUNSELLOR:

Now, we tend to see clients in blocks of six

sessions...

DAVID:

Six?! I was hoping we could sort this out tonight.

COUNSELLOR:

You may find it takes a little longer.

KAREN:

(TO DAVID) Particularly if you keep interrupting.

COUNSELLOR:

Now, perhaps we should start by you each telling me why

you're here.

DAVID:

(MUTTERING SARDONICALLY BUT LOUD ENOUGH FOR THE OTHERS

TO HEAR)   Duress?

THE COUNSELLOR SMILES WANLY AT KAREN.

COUNSELLOR:

Mrs Marsden, would you like to begin?

KAREN:

Well, David and I...

DAVID SENSES IT'S CRUNCH TIME. HE LOOKS FOR A DISTRACTION
AND FINDS THE COUNSELLORS DIPLOMA ON THE WALL.

DAVID:

(INSPECTING DIPLOMA)   American degrees are valid here,

are they?

KAREN IS DISTRACTED BY DAVID'S INTERRUPTION. THE COUNSELLOR
LOOKS AT HER ENCOURAGINGLY - "GO ON".

KAREN:

Erm, I suppose we started having problems...

DAVID:

Does anyone mind if I open a window?

COUNSELLOR:

(BEGINNING TO LOSE HER PROFESSIONAL CALM)   Mr Marsden!

Please!   (TO KAREN)   You were saying.

DAVID'S AMBLING HAS TAKEN HIM BEHIND THE COUNSELLOR'S CHAIR.
HE SPOTS THE BUTTON ON THE WALL MARKED 'ALARM'. FURTIVELY
LOOKING ABOUT, HE REALISES THIS AFFORDS HIM HIS BEST CHANCE
OF SCUPPERING THE SESSION. SURREPTITIOUSLY, HE PRESSES THE
BUTTON

KAREN:

Yes, I think our problems began...

A LOUD ALARM STARTS BLARING. DAVID PICKS UP THE LARGE FIRE
EXTINGUISHER FROM THE FLOOR.

Cold Feet – the best bits...

AMENDED 01/05/98

DAVID:

Fire alarm! Let's keep calm! Evacuate the building!

THE COUNSELLOR HANGS HER HEAD IN HER HANDS.

COUNSELLOR:

That's not the fire alarm. It's a panic button.

AND SURE ENOUGH, AS DAVID GRAPPLES WITH THE FIRE
EXTINGUISHER TO REMOVE THE HOSE FROM HE BARREL, WE HEAR
RUNNING FOOTSTEPS APPROACHING. THE DOOR IS SUDDENLY FLUNG
OPEN AND TWO MALE COLLEAGUES OF THE COUNSELLOR BURST OPEN
INTO THE ROOM. IN A SECOND THEY TAKE IN THE SCENE, AND WE
SEE WHAT THEY SEE - THE COUNSELLOR LOOKING LOST, KAREN
LOOKING SHOCKED, AND MOST SIGNIFICANTLY, DAVID STANDING OVER
THE COUNSELLOR, BRANDISHING THE FIRE EXTINGUISHER IN AN
APPARENTLY THREATENING MANNER. PRESUMING THEIR COLLEAGUE TO
BE IN DANGER, THE TWO MEN *HURL* THEMSELVES AT DAVID, KNOCKING
HIM TO THE GROUND. HE SQUEALS AS HE GOES DOWN, AND
COMPLAINS LOUDLY AS HE'S PINNED TO THE FLOOR.

MALE COLLEAGUE:

(CONCERNED) Are you alright, Janet?

COUNSELLOR:

(TO KAREN * **SYMPATHETICALLY) Has it been very**

difficult? (being married to your husband)

CUT TO

END OF ACT ONE

Director Nigel Cole:

'One of my favourite scenes to do was the flashback in episode five to when Pete and Adam were kids playing football. The kids wore wigs and it was all very late 1970s. The casting department went round the local schools and did a terrific job, coming up with two lads who could have been a young John Thomson and a young Jimmy Nesbitt. Actually, John didn't think the boy we chose looked like him, but everyone else on the crew thought he was a dead ringer. And the lad who played the young Adam did a great eyebrow thing, which is very Jimmy Nesbitt because Jimmy is known for his eyebrows. This boy could raise one eyebrow independently of the other, which was something I thought Jimmy could do. But for the following scene, when I wanted Jimmy to raise one eyebrow just as the boy had, he couldn't do it – he could only raise both!'

The Scripts

```
SCENE   37 EXT
SET   SCHOOL PLAYING FIELD
DAY   TIME

FLASHBACK

YOUNG PETE:
YOUNG ADAM:
FOOTBALL CAPTAIN:

TEN YEAR OLD SCHOOLBOYS ARE HUDDLED IN TWO EQUAL GROUPINGS –
SIX TO A GROUP.  A SINGLE CHILD STANDS SADLY ALONE.  HE
LOOKS LIKE A YOUNGER VERSION OF PETE.  THE TWO GROUPS ARGUE
ABOUT WHO'S GOT TO HAVE GIFFORD ON THEIR TEAM.  YOUNG PETE
LOOKS MISERABLE.  FINALLY, ONE OF THE TWO CAPTAINS GIVES IN.

                    FOOTBALL CAPTAIN:

    Alright, Gifford.  But you'll have to go in goal.

10 YEAR OLD PETE NODS SADLY, AS IF HE KNOWS IT'S HIS FATE TO
SPEND THE REST OF HIS LIFE PLAYING IN GOAL.

CUT BACK TO
```

Cold Feet – the best bits...

93

James Nesbitt
(Adam):

'The scenes which are the most uncomfortable to do from my point of view are the ones which take hours and hours at a time. With the football flashback, they only used 30 seconds of it on tape, but we spent six hours filming it on a freezing day with kids. Tedium is the worst thing about filming. Another nightmare was the cradle scene in episode one of the first series, where Adam appears outside Rachel's office window with a Mexican band to serenade her on the first anniversary of their having had sex. We were about 40 feet up in this cradle, but the height was no problem. The problem was the song, "Guantanamera". By the time we had finished, we were so sick of that song. It became like a chant gone wrong. It was a chant that would take you away from Buddhism as opposed to into it!'

Director *Nigel Cole*:

'I enjoyed doing the charity ball scene in episode six, partly because all six characters were there, which is always nice, and also because it offered that contrast between powerful drama and high comedy. To my mind, that is one of the secrets of the success of *Cold Feet* and here is a perfect example of it. For at the same time as Rachel is in the loo with Karen, confiding in her that she's pregnant, back in the hall Jenny is letting off a fire extinguisher at David's boss, Natalie. So on the one hand, you've got Rachel dropping this bombshell, and on the other you've got this broad slapstick. The contrast between the two is magical.

'We shot the charity ball sequence over two days at the Masonic Lodge in Manchester and that was an experience in itself because none of us had been inside a Masonic Lodge before. The place had a strange atmosphere. It was very cold and when we went into the inner sanctum room, I found that decidedly weird. And while we were filming, up in the gallery watching us were five Masons in full aprons. That was spooky. But the building was ideal for what we needed. I wanted somewhere with a grand staircase and a balcony – somewhere in which Pete and Jenny would feel intimidated. We hired a crane for the shot from the balcony, looking down the stairs, and that helped give it a sense of occasion. It worked well.

'It was a change to see all the men dressed up and I must say they all scrubbed up well. I particularly liked Jimmy Nesbitt doing his James Bond bit in the mirror as he put on his tuxedo. This group of actors are a very inventive lot and they're always coming up with ideas. There was a line where Jenny was talking about a commercial for Jammy Mouthfuls – "so yummy, they fill your tummy". Fay, Jimmy and John suggested

Cold Feet – the best bits...

95

that, rather than say it, they sing it as a jingle, and it worked better that way.

'The fight between Jenny and Natalie is quite spectacular with the table collapsing. We used special safety drinking glasses made out of sugar so that there was no danger from flying glass and we weakened the table in advance so that it would collapse easily. By giving it a collapsible leg, we knew which way it would fall and that is essential in doing fight scenes. They may look haphazard on screen, but in reality they are carefully choreographed and, as the director, I have to know exactly where things and people are going to land so that I can train the cameras on them. We used stunt doubles for the part of the fight where Jenny and Natalie roll across the table and we filled the fire extinguisher with special foam, which wouldn't be dangerous if it accidentally got in the actors' eyes. The design department showed me a number of fire extinguishers which they had rigged up beforehand, but it took a while before we could find one which actually worked. I said: "It may look right, it may be safe, but the one thing it must do is work." The thing was we could only do the fire extinguisher fight twice because after a drenching, it took so long to re-do Natalie's make-up. There simply wasn't time to do any more takes. But I know Fay enjoyed doing it – in fact, she had been looking forward to it all day.'

Fay Ripley (Jenny):

'I probably went a bit over the top with the fire extinguisher scene, but my excuse is that we couldn't rehearse it properly beforehand. I don't think I was supposed to get any on Natalie's face, but I immediately went straight for her face and got it all over her head. I must stress that Lorelei King, who plays Natalie, is a perfectly nice woman. It was not vindictive at all, but the part called for it! It was very good fun and I love doing all that stuff. I really enjoyed the fight, too. I wanted to get right on in there and I ended up doing more than was expected before the stuntwoman took over. I'm definitely game for a pretend fight.

'Another scene I was particularly proud of was a domestic montage scene where I was the happy-go-lucky wife dealing with life incredibly well. Everything had to happen at exactly the right moment. Toast had to pop out of the toaster, the kettle had to boil. There were about ten different things, at the finish of which I had to whack the end of a spoon so that the sugar cube on it went up in the air at the right height and landed in my teacup. I won't pretend I did it first time, but I didn't need as many takes as I thought I would. When I did it, I was so pleased with myself that I felt like I'd just won an Oscar.'

```
SCENE  6 INT
SET   BALLROOM
NIGHT 2  2000                          -

PETE:
JENNY:

PETE AND JENNY STAND AT THE TOP OF A LARGE STAIRCASE THAT
SWEEPS DOWN INTO THE BODY OF THE HALL.  JENNY LOOKS LOVELY
IN HER FINEST DRESS; PETE LOOKS, WELL, UNCOMFORTABLE IN HIS
TOO SHORT TUX; HE STILL BOASTS A CUMMERBUND.  GUESTS SWEEP
PAST THEM AND DOWN INTO THE BALL.  FROM THEIR VANTAGE POINT,
JENNY AND PETE DRINK IN THE VIEW - A SCENE OUT OF A
CONTEMPORARY JANE AUSTEN NOVEL AS BUTLERS MOVE AMONG THE
GLITTERING GUESTS OFFERING THEM CHAMPAGNE FROM SILVER
SALVERS, A WORLD TO WHICH PETE AND JENNY ARE NOT USUALLY
PRIVY.  JENNY IS IN AWE; PETE IS LESS IMPRESSED.
```

                    JENNY:

    Oh my God!! Isn't it wonderful?! Oh I'm so glad David

    invited us.

PETE TURNS TO FACE HER.

                    PETE:

    One thing I've never got clear. If it was an

    invitation, why did we have to pay?

                    JENNY:

    Don't be churlish. It's for charity.

                    PETE:

    (LOOKING OUT AT GUESTS; CHURLISHLY) Yeah, well that

    woman's tiara could pay off Third World debt.

                    JENNY:

    (STRAINING TO LOOK) A tiara!

JENNY AND PETE GIGGLE AT THE RIDICULOUS EXTRAVAGANCE OF THE
WOMAN'S HEADWEAR.

                    JENNY:

    Oh, Pete, I'm so nervous!

                    PETE:

    Why?! They're no better than us. No different to us.

    Still go to the loo. Still wipe their...

JENNY:

    (CUTTING HIM OFF) Alright, alright. I get your point.

PETE:

    We fit right in.

HE OFFERS JENNY HIS ARM. SMILING (PETE'S SO GOOD FOR HER
CONFIDENCE), SHE TAKES IT. PETE LEADS THEM DOWN THE
STAIRCASE. AN ELEGANTLY DRESSED WOMAN PASSING ON HER WAY
UP, CAN'T HELP NOTICING PETE'S TOO SHORT TROUSERS. HER HEAD
TURNS TO FOLLOW HIM ON THE WAY DOWN; SO DO THOSE OF THE
COUPLE BEHIND HER. PETE DOESN'T FIT IN QUITE AS MUCH AS
HE PERHAPS LIKES TO THINK.

CUT TO

<u>SCENE 7 INT</u>
<u>SET BALLROOM</u>
<u>NIGHT 2 2015</u>

DAVID:
KAREN:
PETE:
JENNY:

DAVID AND KAREN STAND IN THE BODY OF THE HALL, CHATTING TO A
COUPLE OF OTHER GUESTS, WHO THEN MOVE OFF TO 'MINGLE'.
DAVID AND KAREN CLUTCH FLUTES OF CHAMPAGNE. KAREN LOOKS
STUNNING IN HER DESIGNER DRESS, ATTRACTING ADMIRING LOOKS
FROM OTHER GUESTS, MEN AND WOMEN. DAVID IS GLOWING WITH
PRIDE; HE LEANS IN TO SPEAK TO HER.

DAVID:

    Have I told you how wonderful you look?

KAREN:

    (PLEASED) More than once. But don't let that put you

off.

DAVID:

    You look a million dollars.

KAREN:

    You saw the price tag?

DAVID:

    Money well spent. Besides, we can write if off against

tax.

KAREN:

I thought this was a social occasion.

DAVID:

(ACKNOWLEDGING SOMEONE HE KNOWS) Good God, no.

Strictly business. I just hope Pete and Adam don't

embarrass me.

KAREN:

Why should they?

DAVID:

Well, they're hardly the most refined of our friends;

(SPOTS PETE & JENNY THROUGH THE CROWD) Ah, here's Pete

and Jenny now. (GETS A BETTER VIEW OF PETE) Good

grief! What's he wearing?!

KAREN GIVES DAVID A LOOK - "BEHAVE!", THEN TURNS TO GREET
PETE AND JENNY.

CUT TO

SCENE 8 INT
SET BALLROOM
NIGHT 2 2020

ADAM:
RACHEL:
WAITER:

ADAM AND RACHEL, BOTH LOOKING AS THOUGH THEY FIT IN, REACH
THE BOTTOM OF THE WINDING STAIRCASE AND PITCH INTO THE BODY
OF PEOPLE. RACHEL LOOKS ABOUT FOR THEIR FRIENDS; ON THE FAR
SIDE OF ADAM, A PASSING WAITER PROFFERS A TRAY OF CHAMPAGNE.

WAITER:

Champagne, sir?

ADAM:

Oh! Don't mind if I do.

HE TAKES TWO FLUTES, AND OFFERS ONE TO RACHEL. SHE DECLINES
IT.

RACHEL:

I won't.

ADAM:

You can have a couple of glasses!

RACHEL:

Best not.

ADAM:

(SLIGHTLY NARKED) Why did you insist on bringing the

car?!

RACHEL:

I don't mind (driving).

ADAM:

Yeah, but what fun are you going to be?

RACHEL:

Adam, you don't have to be pissed to have fun.

RACHEL WANDERS OFF IN SEARCH OF THEIR FRIENDS.

ADAM:

No. But it helps.

ADAM DOWNS A CHAMPAGNE FLUTE IN ONE, THE REPLACES THE EMPTY
GLASS ON THE TRAY OF A WAITER WHO HAPPENS TO BE PASSING AT
THAT PRECISE MOMENT. CLUTCHING HIS SECOND GLASS HE FOLLOWS
RACHEL.

CUT TO

SCENE 9 INT
SET   BALLROOM
NIGHT 2 2030

DAVID:
KAREN:
PETE:
JENNY:
ADAM:
RACHEL:
WAITRESS:

DAVID AND KAREN STAND CHATTING TO PETE AND JENNY. JENNY,
BEING NERVOUS, IS GULPING BACK THE CHAMPAGNE. SHE SEES A
WAITRESS APPROACHING WITH A TRAY OF GLASSES AND POLISHES OFF
HER GLASS SO SHE CAN SWAP IT FOR A FULL ONE. KAREN SPOTS
ADAM AND RACHEL APPROACHING.

KAREN:

Ah! Here they come!

ADAM AND RACHEL ROCK UP AND EXCHANGE AD-LIBBED KISSES AND
GREETINGS. THE WAITRESS LINGERS TO SEE IF ANYONE NEEDS
CHAMPAGNE; RACHEL TURNS HER DOWN, PETE IS THE ONLY OTHER
PERSON WITHOUT A GLASS.

PETE:

(TO WAITRESS) Is there any beer?

THE WAITRESS IS A BIT THROWN; NO ONE ELSE HAS ASKED HER THIS.

WAITRESS:

Erm... Possibly at the bar?

PETE NODS; RIGHT OH.

ADAM:

(TO PETE) I'll come with you.

THEY HEAD OFF FOR THE BAR; DAVID REGARDS THEM, SLIGHTLY
CONCERNED.

JENNY:

(TO RACHEL) So, how are you doing?

RACHEL:

(LESS THAN CONVINCINGLY) Oh, fine. Fine.

CUT TO

SCENE 10 INT
SET BALLROOM
NIGHT 2 2035
                                AMENDED 01/05/98

PETE:
ADAM:
JULIAN:

PETE AND ADAM (WHO'S CLUTCHING HIS CHAMPAGNE) MAKE THEIR
WAY THROUGH THE THRONG TOWARDS THE BAR.

ADAM:

*Does that have a hem?

PETE:

*Double stitched.

A BLOKE A SIMILAR AGE TO ADAM AND PETE RECOGNISES THEM AS
THEY PASS HIM.

JULIAN:

Pete Gifford! And Adam Williams!

PETE AND ADAM STOP TO SEE WHO'S CALLING THEIR NAME. ADAM
RECOGNISES HIM AS SOMEONE THEY KNEW AT SCHOOL, BUT CAN'T
REMEMBER HIS NAME.

ADAM:

Heyy! Ummmm....

ADAM LOOKS TO PETE FOR HELP - "YOU KNOW, WHAT'S HIS NAME".

PETE:

Yeahh!

PETE CAN'T REMEMBER EITHER; THEIR OLD SCHOOLMATE HELPS THEM
OUT.

JULIAN:

Julian Ayres.

ADAM:

(SHAKING HANDS) Pubes! How are you doing?! -

JULIAN:

Good! Great! I tend to be called Julian now.

ADAM:

Sure! So, what brings you here?

JULIAN:

(POINTING TO A WOMAN TALKING TO SOME OTHER PEOPLE)

Susan. She's an accountant.

PETE:

Wow! You finally got a date?

JULIAN:

A wife! We've been married five years. Got three kids.

ADAM:

(IMPRESSED) Really?!

JULIAN:

How about yourselves?

PETE:

Married too. A baby son.

JULIAN:

(TURNING TO ADAM, MATILY) And let me guess... Divorced?

ADAM:

(SOMEWHAT PUT OUT) Why do you say that?

JULIAN:

(REALISING HIS FAUX PAS) Sorry! Married, then?

ADAM:

(A TAD UNCOMFORTABLY) No.

JULIAN:

(AS IN "MAYBE ONE DAY") Oh well.

AN UNCOMFORTABLE SILENCE ENSUES. JULIAN AYRES'S PARTY
STARTS MOVING TO THEIR TABLE, HE'S HAPPY TO USE THIS
DIVERSION TO BREAK OFF HIS CONVERSATION WITH PETE AND ADAM.

JULIAN:

Anyway, great to see you guys! Maybe catch you later.

HE MOVES OFF TO JOIN HIS WIFE. PETE AND ADAM WATCH HIM GO.

PETE:

(IN SOME WONDER) Pubic Ayres!

ADAM:

(REFERRING TO JULIAN) Twat! (TO PETE) Come on!

ADAM HEADS OFF, TRAILED BY PETE.

CUT TO

```
SCENE  11 INT
SET  BALLROOM
NIGHT 2  2045
```

DAVID:
KAREN:
JENNY:
RACHEL:
PETE:
ADAM:
NATALIE:
BILL:

DAVID, KAREN, JENNY AND RACHEL ARE SITTING AT THEIR TABLE
WITH TWO OTHER GUESTS INVITED BY DAVID - HIS BOSS, NATALIE
AND HER HUSBAND, BILL. THE SEATING PLAN AT THE ROUND TABLE
IS AS FOLLOWS - DAVID, NATALIE, SPACE (FOR ADAM), KAREN,
SPACE (FOR PETE), RACHEL, BILL AND JENNY (WHO'S A BIT
TIPSY). PETE AND ADAM MAKE THEIR WAY TO THE TABLE, PETE
EMPTY HANDED, ADAM BEHIND, HIM STILL CARRYING HIS CHAMPAGNE
FLUTE. BILL, CLUTCHING AN EMPTY CHAMPAGNE BOTTLE, SEES PETE
APPROACHING AND SIGNALS TO HIM.

                    BILL:

    Waiter!

PETE LOOKS ABOUT HIM, WONDERING WHERE SAID WAITER IS.

                    JENNY:

    (TO BILL) Erm. That's my husband.

BILL IS SUITABLY EMBARRASSED. HE RISES TO SHAKE PETE'S HAND.

                    BILL:

    Terribly sorry, old chap. My mistake! Bill Lawrence.

PETE COOLLY SHAKES BILL'S HAND.

                    PETE:

    (COOLLY) A pleasure.

PETE AND ADAM SIT. BILL GETS ANOTHER WAITER'S ATTENTION AND
GIVES HIM THE EMPTY CHAMPAGNE BOTTLE, PRESUMABLY ASKING FOR
ANOTHER.

                    JENNY:

    (TO PETE) I thought you were going to get a pint.

PETE:

You have to pay for it. I mean, bugger that. I'll

drink champagne.

DAVID:

(JOKINGLY) If Jenny's left you any.

JENNY:

(DOING THE INTRODUCTIONS) Rachel's boyfriend, Adam,

and my husband, Pete... This is Bill's wife, Natalie.

She works for David.

NATALIE:

Actually, David works for me. I'm his boss.

JENNY:

(EMBARRASSED) Oh, sorry!

NATALIE:

(PATTING JENNY'S HAND) That's okay, honey. You're

doing just fine.

JENNY IS SLIGHTLY PULLED UP BY NATALIE'S (PERHAPS
UNINTENTIONALLY) CONDESCENDING TONE. PETE NOTICES THE
IMPLICIT PUT-DOWN AS WELL, AND DECIDES HE DOESN'T LIKE BILL
OR NATALIE. A WAITER APPEARS, BEARING ANOTHER BOTTLE OF
CHAMPAGNE.

BILL:

Ah. More champagne! Jenny?

CUT TO

```
SCENE  12 INT
SET  BALLROOM
NIGHT 2  2215
```

DAVID:
PETE:
JENNY:
ADAM:
NATALIE:
BILL:

THE MEAL IS IN FULL FLOW, THE WAITERS CLEARING AWAY THE
PLATES AS PEOPLE FINISH THEIR MAIN COURSES. RACHEL AND
KAREN'S SEATS ARE EMPTY. BILL HAS TURNED ROUND AND IS DEEP
IN CONVERSATION WITH A GUEST ON THE ADJOINING TABLE. JENNY
IS LISTENING TO DAVID'S CONVERSATION WITH NATALIE; DRINK IS
BEGINNING TO TAKE ITS TOLL. ADAM IS LEANING ACROSS TO SPEAK
TO PETE. IT'S THE LADS CONVERSATION THAT WE FOLLOW.

      ADAM:

Why do married people always look down on you if you

aren't married?

      PETE:

Eh?

      ADAM:

Pubes! Treated me like a leper.

      PETE:

Bollocks!

      ADAM:

Well, you would say that; you're married too. You

know, I reckon it's cos married people need to reassure

themselves that they haven't made a dreadful mistake.

That's why you want everyone else to join the same

club. But not everyone wants to.

      PETE:

Most people do.

      ADAM:

Not me.

PETE:

Oh, come on! You're telling me that the thought of

marrying Rachel has never crossed your mind?

ADAM GIVES IT A MOMENT'S THOUGHT.

CUT TO

SCENE 13 INT
SET SUIT & DRESS HIRE SHOP
DAY 0 1430

FLASHBACK

ADAM:
RACHEL:
ASSISTANT:

ADAM, ATTENDED BY A SHOP ASSISTANT, IS TRYING ON HIS TUX IN
A SUIT AND DRESS HIRE SHOP; HE'S ALSO WEARING A CUMMERBUND.
HE'S JUST BEEN TOLD THE COST.

ADAM:

Fifty quid! I want to hire it, not buy it!

ASSISTANT:

That is the cost of hire, sir. Though the cummerbund

is extra.

ADAM:

(TAKING OFF CUMMERBUND) Yeah, well it's naff anyway.

(BEAT) Raich, what do you... (think)?

ADAM LOOKS UP TO SEE RACHEL MOVING ACROSS THE SHOP, PAST A
HEADLESS MANNEQUIN WEARING A WEDDING DRESS. HIS WORDS DIE
IN HIS MOUTH AS RACHEL HAPPENS TO STOP BEHIND THE MANNEQUIN
IN SUCH A WAY THAT IT LOOKS AS THOUGH SHE'S ACTUALLY WEARING
THE DRESS. FOR A BRIEF MOMENT ADAM ENVISAGES HER AS A BRIDE
(ARE THOSE WEDDING BELLS WE HEAR CHIMING IN THE BACKGROUND,
AND THE CHEERS OF RELATIVES?) - HE STARES AT HER IN WONDER
- HE'S NEVER SEEN HER IN THIS LIGHT BEFORE.

CUT BACK TO

SCENE 14 INT
SET BALLROOM
NIGHT 2 2218

ADAM:
PETE:
JENNY:
DAVID:
NATALIE:
BILL:

AS BEFORE. ADAM SNAPS OUT OF HIS REVERIE.

ADAM:

Never!

PETE:

I don't know what your problem is.

ADAM:

It's the assumption that *only* married people are in

lasting relationships. I mean, just cos you and Jenny

are married, doesn't mean you're happy.

PETE:

(IN COUNTER ARGUMENT) But we've just had a baby.

ADAM:

(LEAPING ON THIS) Reason enough!

PETE:

You know why I think you hate the idea of marriage?

Fear. Of failure.

PETE LOOKS POINTEDLY AT ADAM - "I HAVE A POINT, DON'T I?"
THE TRUTH IS HE'S HIT A NERVE. ADAM SEEKS TO DEFLECT THE
CONVERSATION.

ADAM:

(SINCERELY) By the way, nice cummerbund.

THE TACTIC WORKS; PETE LOOKS AT HIS CUMMERBUND, CHUFFED -
"DO YOU REALLY THINK SO?".

CUT TO

SCENE 15 INT
SET LADIES CLOAKROOM
NIGHT 2 2220

KAREN:
RACHEL:

WOMEN WANDER IN AND OUT OF THE CLOAKROOM. KAREN STANDS AT
THE BASINS, CHECKING HER MAKE-UP IN THE MIRROR. A TOILET IS
FLUSHED THEN A CUBICLE DOOR OPENS AND RACHEL JOINS KAREN AT
THE BASINS TO WASH HER HANDS. KAREN LOOKS AT HER.

                    KAREN:

    Can I ask you a personal question?

RACHEL REGARDS KAREN NERVOUSLY, THINKING SHE KNOWS WHAT
KAREN IS ABOUT TO SAY.

                    KAREN:

    Are you suffering from a urinary infection?

RACHEL LAUGHS AND RETURNS TO WASHING HER HANDS.

                    KAREN:

    It's just... I've never known anyone pee as often as

    you. Well, apart from my Grandmother.

                    RACHEL:

    I thought you were going to ask me if I'm pregnant.

                    KAREN:

    (IN AMUSED DISBELIEF) You?!!

RACHEL DRIES HER HANDS.

                    KAREN:

    So are you?

                    RACHEL:

    Pregnant?

                    KAREN:

    ("NO!") Suffering from a urinary infection.

RACHEL:

No! (BEAT) I'm pregnant.

KAREN:

What?!!

RACHEL NODS, HER EYES WIDE.

KAREN:

But, Rachel, that's wonderful! (BEAT; OFF RACHEL'S

LOOK) Isn't it?

RACHEL:

It's not something we'd planned.

KAREN:

Still, you must be delighted.

RACHEL:

(MISERABLY) Must I? And how's Adam going to take it?

KAREN:

You haven't told him yet?

RACHEL:

Well, you know what he's like about children.

KAREN:

He loves children! (BEAT; REALISES THIS ISN'T

COMPLETELY TRUE) Well, other peoples.

RACHEL:

That's the second problem. It might not be his.

YOU CAN PRACTICALLY HEAR THE SOUND OF THE BASIN CRACKING AS
KAREN'S JAW HITS IT. RACHEL PULLS A FACE - OOPS!

CUT TO

```
SCENE   16 INT
SET   BALLROOM
NIGHT 2   2230
```

JENNY:
PETE:
ADAM:
DAVID:
NATALIE:
BILL:

BACK AT THE TABLE, THE GUESTS ARE EATING THEIR DESSERTS AS
WAITERS PUT OUT COFFEE CUPS AND AMARETTO BISCUITS (THOSE
ONES IN PAPER WRAPPERS).   JENNY HAS MOVED BEYOND TIPSY AND
ON TO DRUNK.   KEEN TO BE ACCEPTED, SHE'S DESPERATELY TRYING
TO KEEP UP WITH DAVID AND NATALIE'S SHOP TALK.   BEYOND
JENNY, BILL IS ALSO LISTENING IN. KAREN AND RACHEL
ARE STILL IN THE LADIES'; THEIR DESSERTS LIE UNTOUCHED.
ADAM SCANS THE BALLROOM.

                    ADAM:

    (TO PETE) I wonder where the girls have got to.

PETE SHRUGS - BEATS ME.   HIS ATTENTION IS FOCUSSED ON JENNY,
WHO IN HER DRUNKENNESS AND EAGERNESS IS DISPLAYING SOME
WORRYING SIGNS.   HER GAZE DARTS FROM DAVID TO NATALIE, A
MOMENT BEHIND THEIR CONVERSATION.

                    NATALIE:

    (TO DAVID) Okay, it would have to be a hostile

    takeover, but, what the hell?! Wyatt's are vulnerable.

                    JENNY:

    Is this the biscuit people?

                    NATALIE:

    (THROWN) I'm sorry?

                    JENNY:

    Wyatt's Jammy Mouthfuls.

DAVID AND NATALIE REGARD JENNY AS THOUGH SHE'S MAD.   ADAM
AND PETE BOTH LISTEN IN.

                    DAVID:

    Erm... yes, I believe biscuits are part of their food

    manufacturing division. But they're a multinational

    conglomerate.

NATALIE SMILES SWEETLY AT JENNY ("DOES THAT ANSWER YOUR
QUESTION?"), THEN RETURNS HER ATTENTION TO DAVID. -

NATALIE:

Anyway, their last quarter results were really

disappointing. Sales are down and their share price is

at an all-time low.

JENNY:

"So yummy you'll fill your tummy!"

NATALIE:

(BEGINNING TO LOSE HER PATIENCE) What?!

JENNY:

That's their new advertising slogan. I just thought it

might explain why sales are down.

NATALIE:

(NOT BOTHERING TO HIDE HER CONDESCENSION) I expect

it's a *little* more complicated than that.

JENNY:

Ooooh! Pardon me for having an opinion.

NATALIE:

(RUDELY) Look, why don't you have another glass of

champagne and leave us to talk business, okay?

JENNY LOOKS STUNG. PETE DECIDES IT WOULD BE A GOOD IDEA TO
TRY AND CAUSE A DIVERSION BEFORE THINGS GET OUT OF CONTROL.
HE GRABS AN AMARETTO BISCUIT OFF THE TABLE AND UNWRAPS IT.

PETE:

(LOUDLY, TO WHOLE TABLE) Did you know, if you set

light to one of these, it floats up to the ceiling?

DAVID:

(NERVOUSLY) Pete, I'm not sure that's such a good idea.

JENNY IS OBLIVIOUS; HER GAZE IS FIXED HOSTILELY ON NATALIE.

JENNY:

If companies listened to consumers more, they wouldn't

find themselves in such problems.

NATALIE:

(SARCASTICALLY) Oh! A housewife with a Masters in

Business!

JENNY LOOKS FIT TO STRANGLE NATALIE, WHO LOOKS AS THOUGH
SHE'D LOVE JENNY TO MAKE THE ATTEMPT. DAVID LOOKS ANXIOUSLY
FROM ONE TO THE OTHER, THEN QUICKLY AT PETE.

DAVID:

Pete! Why don't you show us that trick with the

biscuit paper?

CUT TO

SCENE 17 INT
SET LADIES CLOAKROOM
NIGHT 2 2230

RACHEL:
KAREN:

RACHEL AND KAREN ARE LOCKED DEEP IN CONVERSATION, OBLIVIOUS
TO THE OTHER WOMEN USING THE BASINS.

KAREN:

Kris?! Your ex-husband?! But you only saw him again

to get a divorce!

RACHEL:

Negotiations proved a bit more complex than anticipated.

KAREN:

I'll say. So when did it happen?

RACHEL:

The first night. He had nowhere to stay so I invited

him back. We were both drunk. Me in particular. In

fact, I'd just thrown up over him.

KAREN:

And he saw that as a come on?!

RACHEL:

It *was* kind of romantic.

CUT TO

SCENE 18 INT
SET ADAM & RACHEL'S BEDROOM
NIGHT 2200

FLASHBACK

RACHEL:
KRIS:

RACHEL AND KRIS SIT ON THE BED AS RACHEL HELPS KRIS OUT OF
HIS VOMIT-STAINED SHIRT.

RACHEL:

(EMBARRASSED) Sorry.

KRIS SMILES FORGIVINGLY AT HER. RACHEL CAN'T HELP NOTICING
WHAT LOVELY EYES HE HAS. OVER THIS IMAGE WE HEAR KAREN'S
VOICE.

KAREN OOV:

Hang on! Excuse me!

> **NB KAREN'S V/O
> RX'D IN SC 19**

CUT TO

SCENE 19 INT
SET LADIES CLOAKROOM
NIGHT 2 2232

KAREN:
RACHEL:

KAREN AND RACHEL AS BEFORE.

> **NB RX KAREN'S V/O
> FOR SC 18**

KAREN:

How come you were in your bedroom?

RACHEL:

I was going to give him one of Adam's shirts to wear.

A BEAT. KAREN IS CONSIDERING WHETHER THIS EXPLANATION IS
ACCEPTABLE. DECIDING IT IS, SHE GESTURES WITH HER HAND TO
INDICATE THAT RACHEL SHOULD PROCEED WITH THE STORY.

CUT BACK TO

SCENE 20 INT
SET ADAM & RACHEL'S BEDROOM
NIGHT 2200

FLASHBACK

RACHEL:
KRIS:

KRIS AND RACHEL AS BEFORE. RACHEL IS HOLDING KRIS'S SHIRT.
THEY'RE BOTH STARING INTO EACH OTHER'S EYES.

KRIS:

This reminds me of Florence.

RACHEL CASTS HER MIND BACK.

RACHEL:

No, my problem then was diarrhoea.

KRIS:

(SMILES - "NOT THEN") When we got caught in that

thunderstorm.

RACHEL:

And hid in the bus shelter?

KRIS:

(NODS) We were soaked through. I took my shirt off.

RACHEL:

So did I.

KRIS:

And then we made love.

THEY LOOK AT EACH OTHER A MOMENT, THEN KRIS STARTS
UNBUTTONING RACHEL'S SHIRT. SHE LETS HIM, KNOWING WHERE
THIS IS LEADING.

CUT BACK TO

```
SCENE  21 INT
SET  LADIES CLOAKROOM
NIGHT 2  2232
```

KAREN:
RACHEL:

KAREN AND RACHEL AS BEFORE.

                    KAREN:

    In a bus shelter?!

                    RACHEL:

    ("IT WAS NO BIG DEAL") It was in Italy. It was (AS IN

    WILD) crazy! It was passionate!

                    KAREN:

    And the last time?

                    RACHEL:

    That was (AS IN 'I MUST HAVE BEEN MAD') crazy!

    (GRIMACES) And passionate. You know I've never really

    got over him.

                    KAREN:

    (CRITICALLY) But he got over you.

RACHEL WINCES - "UNFORTUNATELY".

                    KAREN:

    Where was Adam?

                    RACHEL:

    On his way home. (RUEFULLY) He nearly caught us.

                    KAREN:

    Wow! (BEAT) And you didn't even take precautions?

                    RACHEL:

    Well, I locked the front door.

                    KAREN:

    No! I mean...

*AMENDED 01/05/98**

                    RACHEL:

Oh! No. It all happened so fast.

                    KAREN:

(JOKING) Usually does when they're drunk. So you think
Kris is the father?

                    RACHEL:

Could be. Could be Adam. I mean, condoms aren't
completely reliable.

                    KAREN:

(IN AGREEMENT, LIGHTLY) Man-made. So, what are you
going to do?

                    RACHEL:

I don't know. It's still early days. I might decide
not to go ahead with it.

KAREN GIVES RACHEL A FIXED LOOK - "WHAT EXACTLY DO YOU MEAN
BY THAT?"

                    RACHEL:

Well, I could have a termination.

                    KAREN:

*You mean an abortion.

RACHEL LOOKS MISERABLE.

                    KAREN:

Look, before you decide what to do, go for a scan. It'll
give you a better idea of when you conceived. Kris was
a one-off, right?

                    RACHEL:

("OF COURSE HE WAS!") Yes!

                    KAREN:

Then hopefully a scan will rule him out.

RACHEL LOOKS TROUBLED, AS THOUGH SHE COULDN'T HOPE FOR
ANYTHING HARDER.

CUT TO

SCENE 22 INT
SET BALLROOM
NIGHT 2 2240

DAVID:
PETE:
ADAM:
JENNY:
KAREN:
RACHEL:
NATALIE:
BILL:

A WAITER WITH A FOAM EXTINGUISHER IS TRYING TO CONTAIN THE
SMALL BLAZE THAT PETE'S PARTY TRICK HAS STARTED, SETTING
FIRE TO THE TABLE. HIS PLOY HAS AT LEAST DEFLECTED JENNY AND
NATALIE FROM THEIR ARGUMENT. LIKE THE TABLE'S OTHER
OCCUPANTS, THEY'VE LEAPT BACK TO AVOID THE FLAMES AND ARE
NOW WATCHING THE WAITER'S EFFORTS TO EXTINGUISH THE FIRE -
JENNY TOTTERING SLIGHTLY. NATALIE LEANS IN TO HER HUSBAND,
BILL. SHE TRIES TO SPEAK SOTTO VOCE, BUT HER AMERICAN
ACCENT DOES NOT LEND ITSELF TO LOW VOLUME.

                    NATALIE:

    (TO BILL) I thought the *wife* was stupid! The husband

    appears to be missing a chromosome.

THIS INSULT, HEARD BY ALL AND SUNDRY, IS TOO MUCH FOR JENNY
IN HER TIRED AND EMOTIONAL STATE. SHE GRABS THE FOAM
EXTINGUISHER OUT OF THE HANDS OF THE WAITER AND WITH A CRY
OF...

                    JENNY:

    You bitch!

...UNLOADS ITS REMAINING CONTENTS OVER NATALIE. NATALIE
SCREECHES AND SLAPS JENNY ACROSS THE FACE. JENNY THROWS THE
EXTINGUISHER ASIDE AND GRABS NATALIE BY THE HAIR. THEY
GRAPPLE, PITCHING INTO THE TABLE AND SENDING IT OVER. THEY
CRASH TO THE FLOOR AMID A SHOWER OF CROCKERY. OTHER GUESTS
GATHER ROUND TO WATCH THE FUN. PETE AND DAVID TRY TO DRAG
THE WOMAN APART, AND FINALLY SUCCEED. NATALIE RISES TO HER
FEET. WAITERS UPRIGHT THE TABLE AND CHAIRS AND START BRUSHING
UP THE BROKEN CROCKERY.

                    NATALIE:

    Bill! Come on!

SHE MARCHES OFF, TRAILED BY HER HUSBAND. PETE HELPS JENNY
TO HER FEET.

PETE:

(TO DAVID, EMBARRASSED)   Maybe we'd better be going as well.

DAVID, TOO MORTIFIED TO SPEAK, JUST NODS.   PETE HELPS A SOBBING JENNY AWAY.   ADAM RESUMES HIS SEAT, AND SMILES REASSURINGLY AT DAVID, TRYING (IN VAIN) TO PRETEND THAT THE SITUATION IS NOT HORRIBLY EMBARRASSING.   DAVID SITS, AND HANGS HIS HEAD IN HIS HANDS.   RACHEL AND KAREN RETURN FROM THE LOOS, TO FIND ADAM AND DAVID ALONE AT THE TABLE, WHICH IS BARE SAVE FOR A CHARRED AND STAINED TABLE-CLOTH.

KAREN:

(CHEERFULLY)   Is everyone dancing?

ADAM PULLS A FACE AT KAREN AND RACHEL - "BEST LEAVE IT". DAVID DOESN'T LOOK UP.

CUT TO

Executive producer Christine Langan:

'I'm extremely attached to episode six of series one, partly because it was so difficult to come up with the ending. It was one of those situations where the more troublesome a thing is, the more loved it is. The lynchpin of the entire *Cold Feet* premise was the relationship between Adam and Rachel, and here we were having to decide what on earth to do with them – to keep them together or split them up. It was a big emotional ride.

'Mike Bullen and I discussed from the outset that we wanted to separate Adam and Rachel at the end of series one. We felt the most obvious thing in the world was to have them happily ensconced and that had a feelgood factor to it, but it didn't have much dramatic interest. Whereas if you separated them, viewers would be left asking what on earth happens to them, what happens next? It's a good tag for a second series. But if we had just left them all living happily in their homes in Didsbury, there would be a less compelling reason to revisit them. We knew we'd be setting up some pretty difficult things for ourselves to solve in series two, but that's fun in this business – to give yourself a tricky dilemma to climb out of.

'With *Cold Feet*, we sort of storyline the whole series but additionally, we try to be spontaneous and fresh. It means we are chasing our tails most of the time – a kind of kick-bollock scramble is a fairly accurate description of our methodology. Although it places enormous stresses and strains on our production team, up to a point I do agree with a level of spontaneity in making the story. If a good or better idea comes at you at any point of the process, you should be alive to it. As I say, fairly early on Mike and I decided that we wanted to see Adam and Rachel split by the end of that series, and the more we showed them being in love, the more compelling was the desire to split them. Andy wanted them to stick together – he wasn't sure that splitting them up was the right thing. In the end, Mike and I felt almost cruel in our desire to see them split up. I think I wavered a little at one point and said that maybe we should get them back together, that it was just too bitter an ending.

'Mike, director Nigel Cole and I debated the ending hotly, fiercely and thoroughly. We tried to work out what two people would do in that situation. At the same time, we didn't want Rachel to be desperately unsympathetic as a character. It was all thrashed out over a long Easter weekend. Nigel and I were scratching our heads because he was still lacking an ending to episode six. Nigel and I came up with an idea that Adam would leave town and Rachel would pursue him and make a grand gesture towards him – as grand as his towards her with the rose in the pilot show. We had notions of her talking over the PA on the train and maybe singing – all terribly cheesy. Mike wasn't sure. We batted him a tricky task. We said: give us an ending, make it good and you've got three days! So he locked himself away over the Easter weekend and came up with the ending pretty much as it is. We were thrilled because we knew it was going to be very bittersweet. Mike is brilliant in a corner like that.

'One of the things I love about episode six is that we were able to do a flashback to episode two, where Rachel admits to a horrified Adam that she has been married before. I remember when we shot episode two, discussing with Mike the possibility of using that piece of baggage as something to come back to. When I first started at Granada, I used to work in a soap and I remember a writer talking about treasure in heaven. Basically, if you sow these seeds early enough, you can come back to them. Sure enough in episode six, good old Kris with a "K", the ex-husband, came in handy with Rachel's revelation of her pregnancy. So there's her boyfriend saying he doesn't care whose baby it is, but the truth of her emotional situation is that she knows he doesn't mean it and that he does care. She susses that out, so she has to go.

'It is quite a complex scene, switching as it does from present to past, reality to fantasy, but it is one of which I am extremely proud. The movement between real time and Adam's desperate chase to catch Rachel at the station is intercut with a removal into a fantasy evocation of that same journey, using the Rachmaninov theme from *Brief Encounter*. In a funny way, the tone of that movement and reference from present-day dilemma for our two main characters and the shared experience of the poignancy of *Brief Encounter*, I thought was really subtle and sophisticated. I was especially impressed with the way our director for that episode, Nigel Cole, handled the transitions from reality to fantasy. In someone else's hands they could have been very difficult, but Nigel handled this particularly sensitive moment in our characters' lives with real dramatic dexterity, delicacy, subtlety and charm. Adam's descent from shock and unhappiness through real gut-wrenching pain, loss and sorrow in the knowledge that Rachel is leaving town is beautifully evoked.

'We see Adam driving over a hump-backed bridge with a face of extreme determination and we cut from that to him running onto a station platform. Then we descend into the *Brief Encounter* theme and he catches Rachel just as she is about to go. It's as if he is working out in his head as he is driving to the station exactly what he is going to say to her. Everything he says seems to ring the right note with her

and is sufficient in its passion to make her change her mind about leaving, but just at the last minute as she is trying to undo the door of the train and come away with him, it seems to get jammed. And there's this *Brief Encounter*-type, tragic poignancy as she can't get off the train to join him. A huge cloud of white smoke surrounds his head and, as he becomes engulfed in this, he's desolate. He's cut off from her by this white smoke and from there we cut to a very small Jimmy Nesbitt sliding into frame through a modern station

concourse. We see the arrivals and departures board and Adam's panicked face. He has an altercation with the station master, leaps over the barrier – illegally – and there once again we are in the same moment, but this time it's the present day. *The Brief Encounter* illusion has been dropped. We're suddenly in the crass

reality of 1998. Adam runs down the platform and finds Rachel, but now his word-for-word, passionate plea falls on deaf ears, or at least it fails to persuade her from her course of action. She's going to leave him, she's determined. She finds his Achilles' heel, which is that if he knew that the child she was carrying wasn't his, would he still feel the same? He falters for a moment and that's enough. That's all it takes for her to feel more resolved than ever in her difficult decision. She climbs back onto the train and it disappears into the distance. We see Adam looking forlorn and vulnerable, and he's joined by his best mates, Pete and Jen, who lead him away. And that's it.

'To me, it's a really filmic and gripping sequence. When you hear the first strains of Rachmaninov's music, as a viewer you think: how can they abandon us now? You think it's a cop-out and that the whole thing is going to descend into some kind of parody. But in actual fact, as time passes you realize that Adam and Rachel are going to be no more successful than Trevor Howard and Celia Johnson. *Brief Encounter* has a desperately sad ending and the strains of Rachmaninov should alert us to the fact that it isn't going to go so well. But it's only a fantasy. Then you get the contemporary version and you think: thank God, it's all going to be OK. But it's not. To my mind, it's a rather cheeky bit of drama because it's a way of stalling and playing with anticipation at precisely the moment when you really want to get to the end and see what happens.

'For me, it is one of the most serious notes that we ever play in *Cold Feet,* but it sums up why I love working on the series. I love *Cold Feet* for being a comedy drama where one is allowed and able to explore the more dramatic events in all their seriousness, as well as maintaining a level of humour. You take the characters – in this case, Adam – seriously, so when they make you laugh, it's with a degree of gravity. *Cold Feet* doesn't associate humour and wit and comedy with lightness so much as with truth. And the best comedy will always be about truth and observation.

'The production team really went to town on recreating the 1940s. The whole scenario was very lovingly devised by the designers. We shot the *Brief Encounter* scenes at a steam railway near Rochdale. Nigel filmed most of that with the main unit, but myself and the second unit had to do the shot of the train leaving. It was the very last day's filming of the series and we didn't have a shot of the train disappearing into nothingness. It wasn't that there was a mistake, because we had agreed that Nigel would offload certain shots onto the second unit to augment the very important climax to the whole series. So we went back to the engineers, who were incredibly helpful, and asked whether they could run the engine down the track for us again. It's not always easy to get permission, particularly at short notice, since it is a working steam railway. The carriage we used was just a shell. It was only painted one side – the side we saw to camera. Anyway, they very kindly ran it down the track and we shot it a couple of times and then my mobile phone rang. It was the main unit, telling me they had wrapped the whole series. It was a very moving moment and they all cheered down the phone. Then we all got ready for our wrap party ...'

Writer Mike Bullen:

'The ending to series one was a nightmare. Early on, I had decided that I wanted to do a downbeat ending because people wouldn't expect it, and we like to try and surprise people. I had the idea that Rachel, pregnant but not knowing who the father is, should leave because she felt she had to see the outcome before allowing Adam to commit. Christine and Nigel were both very keen on this, but Andy was less confident. He felt the audience might feel cheated because they were wanting a happy ending, but to his credit he allowed us to go with it because we were all so behind it. So I wrote a draft or two, but it just wasn't working. The motivation wasn't convincing – it didn't hit the right notes. You didn't believe it and it just felt flat. We were getting pretty close to production so there was a lot of pressure on me and I couldn't get it right. Ultimately, because it was getting late in the schedule and I was struggling, Christine and Nigel actually started getting cold feet. We wondered whether we shouldn't, after all, go for the happy ending. At one point they suggested an alternative ending that it should be Adam who leaves because he can't bear the situation and that Rachel should climb onto the train on which he's leaving and sing to him over the tannoy "I've Got You Under My Skin", which was a reprise to the pilot.

'I was horrified. I thought it was an atrocious idea – precisely what we were trying to get away from. But it was useful because it helped to focus my mind on precisely what I was trying to say. We had spent hours and hours talking it through so I just decided to go up to Manchester, lock myself in a room and write it. I wrote the draft in three days over the Easter break and happily that was the one that cracked it and the one they shot. I must admit there was a point where I was beginning to doubt myself, but credit to my wife because, while everyone else was wobbling, she was the one who said: "No, this is absolutely the right storyline." Happy endings are sometimes a cop-out and not necessarily true to life. Life isn't generally that clear-cut. But that scene is so powerful because it is so well directed and brilliantly acted, especially by Jimmy Nesbitt. Now, whenever I watch back episodes, that's the bit which gives me most pleasure and satisfaction.

'I think the *Brief Encounter* image was Nigel's idea. I remember that came out in a meeting and Christine was very enthusiastic. I thought it sounded right and made a note to watch the film because I'd never seen the bloody thing. So I rushed down to the video shop to get *Brief Encounter*. Then I knew what they were talking about. It was good; I enjoyed it.'

Executive producer *Andy Harries*:

'A storyline that promoted enormous discussion between Christine, Mike and myself was Rachel's pregnancy and what was going to happen to the baby. Even while we were filming episode six, we were still discussing whether to keep the baby, have a miscarriage or an abortion. It was very tricky to work out what to do. I was concerned by the abortion. I thought it was very down and I was worried about the effect it would have on Rachel and what people would think of Rachel. But Christine won me round in the end because I think it was braver and more realistic. It would have been a cop-out to have had a miscarriage. The abortion story was much more interesting and challenging to do, involving as it did issues of race. We have always striven to look at a storyline and see how we could make it more interesting, more real, more challenging. I don't think this show has ever suffered from complacency, and I hope it never does. I think you need to surprise your audience continually. That's why it has been so successful. There's not a weary familiarity when *Cold Feet* comes on.'

Helen Baxendale (Rachel):

'The station scene was a great way to end the series. It was funny, irreverent, but also very touching and very cleverly written. That's the thing about *Cold Feet* – it's funny, but it also manages to say something about everyday life. You like the characters because they're all like people you know.'

The Scripts

```
SCENE  77 EXT
SET  MANCHESTER STREETS
DAY 7  1900                              -

ADAM:

ADAM'S CAR TEARS THROUGH THE MANCHESTER STREETS.  ON HIS
FACE HE WEARS A LOOK OF GRIM DETERMINATION.  AS HE SPEEDS
ALONG WE CLOSE IN ON HIS EYES AND SEE WHAT HE'S IMAGINING.

CUT TO
```

```
SCENE  78 INT
SET  OLD RAILWAY STATION
DAY 7  2200                                    -
```

FANTASY

ADAM:
RACHEL:

ADAM RUNS ALONG THE PLATFORM WHERE A TRAIN IS ALL SET TO
DEPART, STARING INTO THE CARRIAGE WINDOWS.

                    ADAM:

   (CALLING) Rachel?! Rachel?!

ADAM IS DRESSED IN HIS PRESENT DAY CLOTHES, BUT OTHER
DETAILS OF THIS FANTASY RECALL ANOTHER ERA - THE MUSIC TELLS
US WHICH - THAT OF "BRIEF ENCOUNTER". THE TRAIN IS OF THAT
VINTAGE; SO TOO IS THE CLANGING BELL, THAT CAN BE HEARD IN
THE BACKGROUND. IN RESPONSE TO ADAM'S CALLING OUT, A WINDOW
IS ROLLED DOWN AND RACHEL'S HEAD APPEARS.

                    RACHEL:

   (EXCITEDLY - "HE'S COME FOR ME!") Adam?!

AN OFF SCREEN RAILWAY GUARD IS HEARD ROUNDING UP THE LAST
PASSENGERS.

                 RAILWAY GUARD OOV:

   All aboard! All aboard now please!

ADAM ARRIVES AT RACHEL'S WINDOW. THE GUARD BLOWS HIS
WHISTLE, LONG AND LUSTY.

                    ADAM:

   Rachel! Don't go. Stay! I don't care whose baby it

   is. I'll be its father.

THE TRAIN SLOWLY STARTS TO MOVE OFF. STEAM BILLOWS UP FROM
BELOW ADAM'S FEET.

                    RACHEL:

   Oh, Adam! Do you mean that?!

ADAM IS NOW HAVING TO WALK ALONG TO KEEP PACE WITH THE
TRAIN. AN OLD RAILWAY WHISTLE IS HEARD. MORE STEAM BILLOWS.

ADAM:

Yes. Yes! Anything so long as we're together↳

THE "BRIEF ENCOUNTER" MUSIC RISES TO A CRESCENDO AS RACHEL
ATTEMPTS TO THROW OPEN THE CARRIAGE DOOR. IT'S STUCK. SHE
LOOKS FRANTICALLY AT ADAM. HE JOINS HER IN WRESTLING WITH
THE DOOR, HAVING TO RUN ALONGSIDE AS THE TRAIN GATHERS PACE.
HE EMITS A STRANGLED CRY AS HE FAILS TO KEEP PACE WITH THE
ACCELERATING TRAIN, AND WATCHES IMPOTENTLY, AS IT STEAMS OUT
OF THE STATION, RACHEL CRYING OUT OF THE WINDOW...

RACHEL:

Adam! Adam! Adam!

ADAM STANDS ON THE PLATFORM, DUMBSTRUCK. OVER THIS IMAGE
WE HEAR THE RAILWAY GUARD'S VOICE.

RAILWAY GUARD OOV:

Oi! Oi!! Where do you think you're going?...

CUT TO

SCENE 79 INT
SET PICCADILLY STATION
DAY 7 1910

ADAM:
RACHEL:
RAILWAY GUARD:

BACK TO REALITY. ADAM, RUNNING TOWARDS A PLATFORM, IS
CALLED BACK AT THE GATE BY AN OFFICIOUS RAILWAY GUARD (THE
SAME VOICE THAT CALLED OUT "ALL ABOARD" IN THE LAST SCENE.
ADAM PAUSES TO ADDRESS THE MAN - A FATAL ERROR.

RAILWAY GUARD:

Let's see your ticket.

ADAM:

I haven't got one.

RAILWAY GUARD:

(INDICATING) Ticket office is over there.

ADAM:

But I'm not going anywhere.

RAILWAY GUARD:

Not without a ticket, you're not.

THE RAILWAY GUARD PULLS ACROSS A LOW BARRIER, CLOSING
THE PLATFORM.

ADAM:

No, I mean, I just need to see someone who's on the

train.

RAILWAY GUARD:

Only passengers are allowed on the platform.

ADAM LOOKS AT THE RAILWAY GUARD AND REALISES THERE'S NO
POINT ARGUING WITH THIS JOBSWORTH. IGNORING HIM, ADAM RUNS
TO THE BARRIER AND HURDLES IT.

RAILWAY GUARD:

Oi!!

ADAM RUNS DOWN THE PLATFORM, LOOKING IN WINDOWS FOR RACHEL.
NO MUSIC A LA "BRIEF ENCOUNTER" ACCOMPANIES HIM, RATHER AN
ADENOIDAL RAILTRACK ANNOUNCEMENT OVER THE TANNOY,
ANNOUNCING A DELAY TO A PARTICULAR TRAIN (NOT THE LONDON
ONE).

ADAM:

(CALLING) Rachel! Rachel!

RACHEL'S HEAD APPEARS FROM A WINDOW FURTHER UP THE TRAIN.

RACHEL:

(NOT EXCITED, BUT SURPRISED) Adam?

ADAM RUSHES UP TO HER.

ADAM:

Rachel! Don't go. Stay! I don't care whose baby it

is. I'll be its father.

RACHEL:

(SADLY) Oh Adam! I wanted to go without seeing you.

ADAM:

(A BIT TAKEN ABACK BY THIS) What? Why?

RACHEL:

Because I (NEARLY SAYS "LOVE YOU") ...I hate myself, Adam. I've ruined everything. It could never be the same between us.

ADAM:

I love you! Enough for both of us!

RACHEL:

Enough for three?

ADAM:

Yes! Even if it's his.

RACHEL:

You can't say that.

ADAM:

I can! I just did.

RACHEL:

But you can't mean it.

ADAM:

I do! Really! (WORRIED THE TRAIN MIGHT BE ABOUT TO GO, ADAM PULLS OPEN RACHEL'S DOOR) Please! You have to get off the train.

RACHEL:

(NOT GETTING OFF) It *is* his.

THAT PULLS ADAM UP SHORT. HE'S SPEECHLESS A BEAT.

ADAM:

(FLATLY) Is it?

RACHEL:

You see. You *want* to mean it. But you can't until you know for sure.

ADAM:

Is it his?

RACHEL:

(GETTING OFF THE TRAIN BUT LEAVING HER BAGS ON) I
don't know. But that's the point. Every day I'm
pregnant we'll be wondering. And dreading the moment
of truth. I *can't* go through that, Adam. For the
baby's sake.

RAILWAY GUARD:

(SHOUTING DOWN THE PLATFORM) You're going to have to
close that door now!

RACHEL CLIMBS ONTO THE TRAIN, LEAVING THE DOOR OPEN, AND
LOOKS AT ADAM, WONDERING IF HE UNDERSTANDS. A BEAT, THEN
ADAM CLOSES THE DOOR. RACHEL LEANS DOWN AND THEY KISS. THE
TRAIN STARTS MOVING, TEARING THEIR LIPS APART. ADAM WATCHES
AS THE TRAIN GATHERS SPEED. HE DOESN'T WAVE, AND NEITHER
DOES RACHEL. THEY JUST WATCH THE DISTANCE GROWING BETWEEN
THEM.

                    ADAM:

    (QUIETLY) But I love you.

THE TRAIN EXITS THE STATION AND DISAPPEARS FROM VIEW. ADAM
STANDS, WATCHING THE SPACE WHERE THE TRAIN HAD BEEN.
FINALLY, HE TURNS.. TO FIND JENNY AND PETE WALKING TOWARDS
HIM. HE LOOKS AT THEM IN SHOCK.

                    ADAM:

    She's gone.

JENNY NODS SADLY - SHE THOUGHT SHE MIGHT.

                    PETE:

    Come on, mate. Let's go home.

ADAM NODS - THERE'S NOTHING ELSE TO DO. WITH ADAM IN THE
MIDDLE AND WITH PETE AND JENNY'S ARMS ROUND HIM, THEY WALK
AWAY.

FREEZE FRAME OR FADE TO BLACK

END OF EPISODE SIX

Director Tom Hooper:

'One of the best things about *Cold Feet* is the way it inter-cuts fantasy and reality. A good example of this is the canal sequence at the start of the second series. It's six months after the pregnant Rachel has walked out on Adam and he and Jenny are walking together along a canal towpath. He's fantasizing about the daughter he might have and there's a flash-cut to his imaginary daughter Amy, an internationally-acclaimed scientist, who has just discovered a cure for cancer. And then we see a flash-cut to Jenny's secret fantasy, which is being on a gondola with Adam, but instead of Venice, the gondola is really on Manchester ship canal. It's that juxtaposition of reality and fantasy, of bringing a character back down to earth. It's a nice way of opening the episode as it shows Jenny's buried desire for Adam, about which he had no idea at that stage.

'Jimmy Nesbitt was stark naked in the gondola apart from a strategically-placed cushion and it was a very cold March day when we filmed it, so I had to get the shot right pretty quickly because Jimmy was freezing. The trouble with gondolas is that they're not easy to steer. We'd set it off in the middle of the canal, but it kept drifing towards the banks and because the setting was supposed to be romantic and perfect, we didn't want the gondola drifing off-course and bumping into the sides. In all, it took about an hour and a half before we got it right, during which time poor Jimmy was on the end of a fair amount of good-natured abuse from onlookers!'

Fay Ripley (Jenny):

'It was about minus 30 when we did the gondola scene. It was cold for me, but worse for Jimmy although I do believe he had a hot-water bottle secreted beneath his heart-shaped cushion.'

James Nesbitt (Adam):

'The gondola scene was freezing, but I was warmed by the presence of Fay. She was warm enough. But like the rose scene from the pilot, it was an enduring image that was worth doing because you know no one else is going to do it. I don't mind doing things like that because they're fun.

'Fay is fantastic to work with – she's an extraordinarily funny person. I've known her for years and she's the most gifted comedienne I've ever known ... by a long way. And she can also play moments of love very well. I really enjoy my bar scenes with John, too because we get to improvise a lot of the dialogue. There's a flexibility which allows us to put little things in. There's a good rapport between John and me. In fact, the whole cast work very well together. I just can't believe how lucky I am to be working on such a great series.'

The Scripts

```
SCENE   13 EXT
SET   CANAL
DAY 1 FANTASY 1600

ADAM:
JENNY:
BOATMAN:

ADAM AND JENNY CRUISE DOWN THE
CANAL ON A GONDOLA.

        ADAM:

Let's get married.

        JENNY:

Okay.


CUT BACK TO SCENE 14 EXT CANAL BANK
```

Director Tom Hooper:

'John Thomson has a great sense of comedy and one scene where he really excels is when Pete is sneaking around the supermarket with a camera, trying to snatch photos of Rachel and a baby. He wants to find out what colour the baby is – to prove whether the father is Adam or Kris – but doesn't know that Rachel is merely looking after a Japanese woman's baby. We shot this at a Morrison's store on a Sunday afternoon and evening. They shut at four o'clock, so we were able to film there between four and midnight. You have to make allowances when working with any children, but especially babies, so we always tend to use more than one to ease the load and stop them getting too tired. The babies we used were fine at first, but by ten o'clock they started bawling, so it became a bit fraught. It's difficult working late with babies.

'You never quite know what you're going to find on night filming. In the same episode is a scene with Adam and Jenny kissing in a multi-storey car park. We had wrapped for the night, and Christine Langan and I were on our way out of the car park when we saw this guy acting strangely. There was something not quite right about him, so we followed him. It turned out he was a potential suicide, who was planning to jump from the top of the car park. Christine and I spent about half an hour trying to talk him down before the police arrived and took over. He came down in the end, but it was bizarre.'

John Thomson (Pete):

'The supermarket scene was a nightmare. It was the first scene we shot of the second series and it went on and on. The poor kids were playing up to the point where the Joshes (we had twins playing David and Karen's son) were replaced halfway through the scene by a blond kid. He was just gold and really behaved himself. It was odd, having the run of a supermarket – there was a great desire to loot!'

SCENE 55 INT
SET SUPERMARKET
DAY 3 1730

PETE:
BABY ADAM:
RACHEL:
Supermarket Extras:

PETE IS PUSHING A TROLLEY
(CONTAINING A SMALL NUMBER OF
ITEMS) ROUND THE SUPERMARKET, HIS
SON ADAM IS STRAPPED INTO A BABY
SEAT; HE CONSULTS A SHOPPING LIST
AS HE GOES. HE FINDS THE SHELF
HE'S LOOKING FOR (BABY FOOD) AND
SCANS ITS PRODUCTS, TAKING TWO TINS
OFF THE SHELF. HE SHOWS THESE TO
THE BABY.

          PETE:

Apple and blueberry or banana and

peach?

BABY ADAM STARES AT PETE BLANKLY.
PETE TAKES ANOTHER TIN OFF THE
SHELF.

          PETE:

Or double chocolate?

BABY ADAM SQUEALS WITH DELIGHT AND
GRINS, WAVING HIS ARMS ABOUT.

          PETE:

(TO HIMSELF AFFECTIONATELY) Like

mother like son.

PETE TOSSES THE TIN INTO THE
TROLLEY. HE LOOKS UP AND HAPPENS
TO GLANCE AT THE END OF THE AISLE
WHERE WHO SHOULD HE SEE BUT RACHEL
WANDERING PAST, ALONE, WITHOUT
SHOPPING BASKET OR TROLLEY. PETE
DOUBLE-TAKES, GOB-SMACKED AND LOOKS
AT BABY ADAM ("DID YOU SEE WHAT I
SEE?"). HE LEAPS INTO ACTION,
QUICKLY SHOVELLING A LOAD OF DOUBLE
CHOCOLATE DESSERTS INTO HIS
TROLLEY, THEN SCAMPERING UP THE
AISLE (COMPLETE WITH TROLLEY) IN
PURSUIT OF RACHEL.

CUT TO SCENE 56 INT SUPERMARKET

SCENE 56 INT
SET SUPERMARKET
DAY 3 1733

PETE:
BABY ADAM:
RACHEL:
KAREN:
JOSH:
Noriko's Baby:
Supermarket Extras:

BABY ADAM SITS DUTIFULLY WATCHING
AS, LIKE A SOLDIER ON MANOEUVRES,
PETE, HIS BACK TO THE SHELF, EDGES
GINGERLY ALONG THE END OF AN AISLE
THEN TENTATIVELY PEERS ROUND. TO
HIS HORROR, HE FINDS HIMSELF INCHES
FROM RACHEL, WHO'S KNEELING DOWN TO
PICK UP A BAG OF NAPPIES FROM LOW
ON A SHELF (AND CONSEQUENTLY
DOESN'T SEE HIM). PETE LEAPS BACK
INTO HIDING, WAITS A BEAT OR TWO,
THEN SLOWLY PEERS ROUND AGAIN.
RACHEL IS NOW HALFWAY DOWN THE
AISLE, PUTTING THE NAPPIES INTO
KAREN'S VERY FULL SHOPPING
TROLLEY. (KAREN STANDS NEARBY;
JOSH SITS IN THE TROLLEY'S CHILD
SEAT). PETE WATCHES AS RACHEL
TURNS AWAY TO ANOTHER TROLLEY
THAT'S NEARBY (AND WHICH CONTAINS A
NUMBER OF BOTTLES OF WINE). HIS
EYES GAPE WHEN HE SEES THAT THIS
TROLLEY ALSO BOASTS A BABY IN ITS
CHILD SEAT, AND HIS EYES WIDEN WHEN
RACHEL TICKLES THE BABY'S CHEEK AND
COOS AT IT. IT MUST BE HERS! (THE
BABY'S FACE IS HIDDEN FROM PETE).

PETE DARTS BACK OUT OF SIGHT AND
JAW GAPING, TAKES IN WHAT HE'S JUST
SEEN. THEN HE CASTS ABOUT,
APPARENTLY LOOKING FOR A PRODUCT OF
SOME KIND. GRABBING HIS OWN
TROLLEY, HE SCAMPERS OFF, AWAY FROM
THE WOMEN, IN SEARCH OF A
PARTICULAR ITEM.

CUT TO SCENE 57 INT SUPERMARKET

SCENE 57 INT
SET SUPERMARKET
DAY 3 1736

PETE:
BABY ADAM:
Supermarket Extras:

PETE AND TROLLEY SKID TO A HALT BY
A SHELF CONTAINING A RANGE OF
DISPOSABLE CAMERAS. PETE SCANS THE
SHELF FOR WHAT HE WANTS - NOT
WIDE-ANGLE, NOT UNDERWATER, AH HA!
HERE IT IS! A DISPOSABLE CAMERA
WITH A FLASH. HE GRABS IT
TRIUMPHANTLY AND RIPS OPEN THE PACK.

CUT TO SCENE 58 INT SUPERMARKET

SCENE 58 INT
SET SUPERMARKET
DAY 3 1738

RACHEL:
KAREN:
JOSH:
PETE:
BABY ADAM:
Noriko's Baby:
Woman:
Supermarket Extras:

RACHEL AND KAREN CHAT AS THEY CHECK
OUT LETTUCES. A WOMAN WALKING
NEARBY LOOKS SUSPICIOUSLY AT A
TROLLEY AS SHE PASSES IT. WITH
GOOD REASON. IT'S PETE'S TROLLEY
AND HE'S CROUCHED BEHIND, USING IT
AS CAMOUFLAGE. HE PEERS THROUGH
THE TROLLEY'S WIRE MESH AND GETS
HIS FIRST GOOD LOOK AT THE BABY -
AND IS CONSIDERABLY TAKEN ABACK TO
DISCOVER ITS ORIENTAL FEATURES.
GETTING A GRIP ON HIMSELF, PETE
QUICKLY SHOOTS OFF A PICTURE OF THE
BABY. THE FLASH GOES UNNOTICED BY
RACHEL AND KAREN.

CUT TO SCENE 59 INT SUPERMARKET

SCENE   59 INT
SET   SUPERMARKET
DAY 3 1740

RACHEL:
KAREN:
JOSH:
PETE?:
BABY ADAM?:
Noriko's Baby:
Cashier:
Supermarket Extras:

RACHEL AND KAREN STAND AT THE
CHECK-OUT, RACHEL PILING THEIR
GROCERIES ON THE COUNTER; KAREN AT
THE OTHER END, BAGGING THEM.
ANOTHER FLASH CAUSES THEM AND THE
CASHIER TO STOP AND LOOK AROUND.
BUT NOTICING NOTHING UNTOWARD, THEY
RETURN TO WHAT THEY WERE DOING.

CUT TO SCENE 60 INT SUPERMARKET DAY

SCENE   60 INT
SET   SUPERMARKET
DAY 3 1742

RACHEL:
KAREN:
PETE:
JOSH:
BABY ADAM:
NORIKO'S BABY:
Supermarket Extras:

RACHEL AND KAREN ARE LEAVING THE
SUPERMARKET. THEY APPROACH A MAN
STANDING NEAR THE ENTRANCE, HIDDEN
BEHIND AND APPARENTLY READING A
BROADSHEET NEWSPAPER. THEY FAIL TO
NOTICE THAT THE PAPER HAS A SMALL
ROUND HOLE TORN IN ITS CENTRE. AS
THE GIRLS NEAR, KAREN'S MOBILE
RINGS. SHE AND RACHEL STOP AS SHE
ANSWERS IT.

                    KAREN:

(INTO PHONE) Hello?... Ah, Noriko!

How's Akira?... Oh, good!...

KAREN SMILES REASSURINGLY AT RACHEL
AND THEY CONTINUE ON THEIR WAY OUT
OF THE SUPERMARKET, PASSING CLOSE
TO PETE. THE NEWSPAPER HIDES THE
FLASH OF HIS CAMERA. ONCE THEY'VE
GONE OUT TO THE CAR PARK, PETE
EMERGES FROM BEHIND THE NEWSPAPER,
CLUTCHING THE CAMERA. HE GRINS
TRIUMPHANTLY AT HIS SON - "YEAH!
GOT IT!"

CUT TO SCENE 61 INT DAVID & KAREN'S
KITCHEN

Executive producer Andy Harries:

'Mike Bullen has a really good ear for natural dialogue and situations, and is an excellent absorber. He can take a lot of ideas on board. Many of the situations in *Cold Feet* are things that Mike, Christine or I have heard about, or experienced, or thought about. One of the most interesting things about being involved in *Cold Feet* is that the three of us have pooled our personal resources into the storytelling, and there are a couple of examples where Mike has brilliantly written ideas based on things that have happened to me. One is the scene in episode one of series two, where David is very preoccupied and goes to pick up his son Josh from school. Having just lost his job, David's mind is elsewhere and he fails to see his little boy wandering off until the last minute, when he rushes in front of a car and snatches him to safety. For David, this incident provokes an important reassessment of his values and of the amount of time he spends with his son.

   'This was not a hugely original idea, but it was something that had once happened to me. I have twin boys and they had gone cycling down a hill in a park when they were about four or five years old. One had shot straight over the handlebars and hit the gravel, and was rushed – by the nanny who was looking after them – to the hospital casualty department. I got a garbled message while I was working in the office that he was quite badly hurt, had a bad head wound and had been rushed into surgery. I got in a cab to rush to the hospital, but it was one of those terrible days when the London traffic was heavy. As I edged my way slowly to the hospital, it provoked a huge rethink about the importance and value of my children and about the priorities in my life. I would say that of all the characters in *Cold Feet*, David is the one I particularly identify with.'

Director Tom Hooper:

'Although on screen it looks as if David is snatching Josh from the path of an oncoming car, when we actually filmed it, there was no car. We shot the scene in two parts – the first with David grabbing Josh, and the second with the car screeching to a halt. The reason for this was that it would have been too dangerous to have expected Robert Bathurst to pick up the boy and land safely when a car was present, too. There were too many factors, too many things to take into consideration to do the whole thing in one go. And we couldn't use a stuntman instead of Robert because there is a close-up on his face.

'What we did was get the police to seal off the street for us and then we erected a large, seven-metre wide, five-metre high, green screen across the street to block out the background. In front of the screen we had our parked cars outside the school, plus our actors. To the side, out of shot, was a crash mat for Robert and the boy to make a soft landing. Then we put the boy in the middle of the street and Robert snatched him up and made his landing. We didn't hang about over this, partly because it was raining and wet patches were starting to appear on our giant screen. And whilst the screen blocks out everything, damp patches would show through and be visible on our background. The other reason we hurried along was because Robert was proving so convincing in his anguish that the boy playing Josh was becoming upset, too. When we were happy with that part, we got rid of the big screen and drove our car up, having it slam on its brakes just short of the spot where David and Josh had been. Finally, we married the two sections together in post-production so that it looked as if it was all done at the same time.'

Robert Bathurst (David):

'We had two-year-old twins playing Josh but for the rehearsal, we used a clothed shop-window dummy. The stuntman rather merrily said: "You run in, grab him under the arms and leap into the air so that you leave the shot parallel to the ground and land on the crash mat." Easy as that! With the dummy, it was just about possible, but with a boy who was twice the weight, one of us would have ruptured our spleen. So I wasn't keen and they thought: "What a wimp – he's not going to be prepared to do this." But in the end I did a messy – but I thought quite realistic – drag out of the way. It was very unchoreographed and as a result looked quite real.

'We got the boy to wander out into the middle of the road by telling him there was a spider there. So he wandered happily in front of this green screen. We made sure that the other twin wasn't watching, but obviously we knew we'd only get two takes. In fact, we only did one take. The boy didn't know he was going to get scooped up and that particular twin started calling me "Horrible Daddy Robert" for the next couple of days.

'In the following episode with the same twins, we had a ten-second sequence of a donkey ride on Blackpool beach. It took three hours to film on the coldest day in Blackpool. The sands were singing and the donkeys – we used two identical ones – were getting more and more cantankerous. As one little boy was being warmed up in the caravan, the other was sitting on the donkey, slowly going hypothermic. Just when we were ready for a take, we'd get the "oven-ready" one out and put him on the donkey, and carry on until the other one was de-chilled. And so the process continued until the donkeys went on strike and we couldn't do any more. All in all, it was a thoroughly miserable day.

'Eventually the twins went on strike, too and we had to get two new twins in. Two-year-olds have minds of their own and they started playing up. They got fed up with being pushed around. They were nice, spirited boys but, quite rightly, said: "No more – I'm not having Horrible Daddy Robert doing that to me!"'

The Scripts

```
SCENE  86 EXT
SET  NURSERY
DAY 7 1800

DAVID:
JOSH:
NATALIE:
Mums & Dads:
Other Children:
Car Driver:

DAVID LOOKS RATHER UNCOMFORTABLE
STANDING OUTSIDE THE NURSERY (HE'S
THE ONLY MAN IN EVIDENCE), AS
CHILDREN RUN OUT TO BE GREETED BY
THEIR MUMS.  JOSH EMERGES AND TROTS
OVER TO DAVID BUT NEITHER EXPECTS AN
EMBRACE NOR RECEIVES ONE, DAVID
INSTEAD PATTING HIM TENTATIVELY ON
THE HEAD AND AD-LIBBING SMALL TALK
("SO HOW WAS YOUR DAY?" ETC).
DAVID LOOKS UP WHEN HE HEARS HIS
NAME CALLED, TO SEE NATALIE RUNNING
TOWARDS THEM.
```

AMENDED 18.3.99
DAVID:

(TO JOSH)   Josh, do you want to

take a biscuit with you?

NATALIE:

(OUT OF BREATH AND EXCITED)   David!

David!

DAVID:

Natalie!

NATALIE:

Karen said I'd find you here. I

just had to see your face when I

told you.

DAVID REGARDS HER.

DAVID:

Told me what?

NATALIE:

Look, I never wanted to

let you go, you were the best member

of my team.   But there were

decisions I had no control over.

So I've quit.

DAVID:

You've quit?! (INCREDULOUS AND

TOUCHED)   Because they let me go?

Get Real David. (ROLLS EYES) Because I couldn't make my own decisions! The thing is, I've been headhunted by DZQ (*pronounced zee*). I want you to come with me.

A BEAT. DAVID CAN'T BELIEVE HE'S BEING OFFERED THIS OLIVE-BRANCH BUT HE'S SAVVY ENOUGH TO MAKE FURTHER ENQUIRIES BEFORE LEAPING AT IT.

DAVID:

What as?

NATALIE:

My number two, naturally.

DAVID:

Salary?

NATALIE:

20% increase and pay review.

DAVID:

Pension?

NATALIE:

Top whack plus share options.

DAVID SMILES AND LOOKS OFF INTO THE MIDDLE DISTANCE, PONDERING HIS GOOD FORTUNE. HIS EYES WANDER TOWARDS THE NEARBY ROAD AND A LOOK OF HORROR ENGULFS HIS FACE AS HE SEES JOSH (WHO HE'D FORGOTTEN ABOUT) CASUALLY WANDERING BETWEEN TWO CARS TOWARDS THE BUSY ROAD.

DAVID:

(SCREAMS) Josh!! No!!

AMENDED 18.3.99

JOSH LOOKS BACK TOWARDS HIS FATHER
AS HE PREPARES TO TAKE ANOTHER
STEP, WHICH WILL TAKE HIM PAST THE
CARS AND OUT INTO THE TRAFFIC.
DAVID LEAPS OVER THE BONNET OF A
CAR AND MANAGES TO SNATCH JOSH BACK
FROM THE JAWS OF DEATH. HE HUGS
THE BOY TO HIS CHEST.

        DAVID:

Oh, my baby! Oh, Josh. My boy!

DAVID SOBS WITH RELIEF, KISSES JOSH
ALL OVER HIS HEAD AND CLINGS
THE CHILD TO HIS BODY AS THOUGH
HE'S SCARED TO EVER LET HIM GO
AGAIN. A SHORT DISTANCE UP THE
ROAD, THE CAR DRIVER HAS STOPPED,
GOT OUT OF THE CAR AND IS LOOKING
BACK - THIS WAS A NARROW ESCAPE.

CUT TO SCENE 87 INT PETE & JENNY'S
LOUNGE

Executive producer Christine Langan:

'Episode two of series two focuses greatly on the increasing attraction between Jenny and Adam, and my favourite scene from that episode is the phone call sequence. Pete has become aware that Jenny is drawn to someone else, but he doesn't know that it's to his best friend. So he asks Adam to leave his mobile phone on so that he can eavesdrop on Adam's conversation with Jenny in the hope of finding out the identity of the mystery man. When Mike Bullen rang me up to say that he had hit on the idea of this phone call, there was a feeling that it was one of those chancy moments which, if not handled subtly, could be unbelievable. But it is the challenge of such moments that makes my job rewarding. Tom Hooper directed it beautifully – and with great subtlety – and there is real potential sitcom in the confusion. My contribution was the suggestion that Adam should stop Jenny's mouth with a kiss. It is the only thing he can think of doing to shut her up, to stop her blurting out his name with Pete listening in, but of course, given the situation, it is just about the worst thing he could have done. You know that Jenny will invoke memories of the stolen kiss to add wood to the flames at a later date. I love the way Adam moves the phone around the table so that Pete can listen in properly and the faces he makes for the benefit of the audience show the frustration of him trying to eke something out of what is a really ugly situation.'

Director Tom Hooper:

'The phone scene was great fun to do – it has so many delicious twists and turns. John and Jimmy suggested moving the phone around the kitchen and that worked really well. It's funny, yet believable. Jenny's incriminating revelations about Adam being downed out by the kettle coming to the boil at precisely that moment might have seemed far-fetched at first, but again it worked in the context of the scene. I think there was a suggestion to use a boiling kettle a second time, but that would definitely have been pushing it too far.'

SCENE 28 INT
SET ADAM'S KITCHEN
NIGHT 1 2036

ADAM:
JENNY:

THE DISPLAY ON ADAM'S MOBILE PHONE
INDICATES THAT THERE'S A CALL IN
PROGRESS. IT'S LYING DISCREETLY ON
A WORK SURFACE NEXT TO THE SINK.
ADAM STANDS NEARBY. JENNY STANDS
ACROSS THE ROOM, SWITCHING ON THE
KETTLE.

ADAM:

So.. why d'you think you're off Pete

at the **minute**?

JENNY:

It's worse than that, **really**.

ADAM:

(TRYING TO GET HER TO TALK LOUDER)

Pardon?

AMENDED 19.3.99
JENNY:

I mean, let's not **sod about here**,

I just don't see in him what

I used to.

ADAM:

(MAKING NO EFFORT TO MOVE CLOSER)

Sorry, can you speak up a bit?

JENNY REGARDS ADAM ODDLY. SHE WALKS
TOWARDS THE WORK SURFACE ON WHICH
IS THE MOBILE PHONE (CAUSING ADAM A
BRIEF MOMENT OF ANXIETY) THEN LOOKS
IN A CUPBOARD ABOVE IT, TAKING OUT
A BOX OF TEA BAGS.

JENNY:

I feel really guilty. I mean, **our**

child's only a year old. But,

you can't dictate when you're gonna

fall out of love, can you?

CUT TO SCENE 29 INT PETE & JENNY'S
LOUNGE

SCENE 29 INT
SET PETE & JENNY'S LOUNGE
NIGHT 1 2037

PETE:
JENNY OOV:
ADAM OOV:

PETE CHOMPS ON A HANDFUL OF
PRINGLES AS HE LISTENS TO THE
PHONE. THROUGH THE PHONE WE HEAR
THE CONVERSATION IN ADAM'S KITCHEN.

     JENNY OOV:

You want tea or coffee?

     ADAM OOV:

Tea please, yeah.

CUT TO SCENE 30 INT ADAM'S KITCHEN

     SCENE 30 INT
     SET ADAM'S KITCHEN
     NIGHT 1 2037

     ADAM:
     JENNY:

     ADAM LEANS AGAINST THE
     WORK-SURFACE; JENNY LOOKS AT THE
     CUPS ON THE SIDE. THEY'RE DIRTY.
     SO SHE LOOKS IN THE CUPBOARDS FOR
     CLEAN ONES.

         ADAM:

     So, there's no particular reason?

         JENNY:

     How do you mean?

         ADAM:

     Oh, I don't know. (SHRUGS - "FOR

     INSTANCE") Someone else?

         JENNY:

     (STOPS SEARCHING; SMILES

     EMBARRASSED) **What makes you say**

      that?

AMENDED 19.3.99
ADAM:

Well, you're an attractive woman.

Even with a child. Any bloke in

his right mind's bound to fancy you.

JENNY:

Do you mean that?

ADAM:

Hell, yes!

A BEAT.

JENNY:

Actually, there is someone else.

CUT BACK TO SCENE 31 INT PETE'S
LOUNGE

SCENE 31 INT
SET PETE & JENNY'S LOUNGE
NIGHT 1 2038

PETE:

A HANDFUL OF PRINGLES STOPS HALFWAY
TO PETE'S OPEN MOUTH AS HE'S
STUNNED BY JENNY'S CONFESSION.

CUT BACK TO SCENE 32 INT ADAM'S
KITCHEN

SCENE 32 INT
SET ADAM'S KITCHEN
NIGHT 1 2038

ADAM:
JENNY:

ADAM STARES AT JENNY. A BEAT.

            ADAM:

Jesus, there is someone else?!

What's he like?

            JENNY:

(COYLY) Well, he's seeing someone

at the moment, but I know that's

not serious. He lives alone. He's

funny. **Really funny.** Quite

good-looking, Just not as much as he

likes to think. Oh and he's not big

on cleanliness. **Have you got any**

  clean mugs?

                        AMENDED 19.3.99
                        ADAM:

            So, does Pete know him?

            JENNY TAKES A COUPLE OF MUGS.

                        JENNY:

            Yeah.

            THE MOBILE PHONE IS NEXT TO THE
            STOVE WHERE THE KETTLE BEGINS TO
            WHISTLE FULL BLAST. JENNY'S VOICE
            IS COMPLETELY DROWNED OUT BY THE
            NOISE.

                        JENNY:

            It's...

            CUT BACK TO SC 33 INT PETE &
            JENNY'S LOUNGE

SCENE 33 INT
SET PETE & JENNY'S LOUNGE
NIGHT 1 2039

PETE:

ALL PETE CAN HEAR THROUGH THE
MOBILE PHONE IS A WATERFALL
DROWNING OUT ALL CONVERSATION. HE
SHAKES THE PHONE, THINKING IT MIGHT
BE STATIC ON THE LINE.

CUT BACK TO SC 34 INT ADAM'S KITCHEN

SCENE 34 INT
SET ADAM'S KITCHEN
NIGHT 1 2039

ADAM:
JENNY:

ADAM STARES AT JENNY, WHO'S USING
WASHING THE CUPS UNDER THE
CASCADING WATER AS A PRETEXT FOR
NOT LOOKING HIM IN THE FACE.

    ADAM:

(CONFUSED) His best friend? But

that's... (LOOKS GOBSMACKED)

JENNY TURNS THE TAP OFF.

    JENNY:

(SMILING EMBARRASSED) That's

right. It's...

ADAM REALISES HE MUST SILENCE
JENNY, AND FAST! SO HE GRABS HER
HEAD AND MASHES HIS MOUTH AGAINST
HERS, CAUSING HER TO SWALLOW HER
WORDS IN WHAT SHE COULD BE MISTAKEN
FOR THINKING IS A PASSIONATE KISS.
THEY BREAK APART. JENNY TOTTERS,
CATCHING HER BREATH. IN THAT
MOMENT, ADAM LEAPS FOR THE MOBILE
PHONE AND (UNNOTICED BY JENNY)
PUNCHES IT OFF. HE SMILES WANLY AT
JENNY; SHE LOOKS FLUSHED.

CUT TO END OF PART ONE

Director Tom Hooper:

'The scene where Pete storms into Adam's office and hits him after finding out that his best friend is Jenny's mystery man is one of the most dramatic in episode two of the second series. Yet at the same time, it is funny because Adam is subjected to this very public embarrassment in a huge, open-plan office. Everything seems so ordered and controlled until Pete marches in and demands to know where Adam Williams is sitting.

'We filmed it at the BT offices in Manchester and the extras were genuine BT employees. Apparently, BT are so sensitive about their equipment that they wouldn't let anyone else in, so we had to use their workforce. But they were great and I think having genuine office workers as opposed to actors added to the reality. I know the guy who shouted at Pete to stop was thrilled to bits at being on TV. It made his day. But the scene was physically exhausting for John Thomson because there was a lot of climbing over desks.'

John Thomson (Peter):

'This is my favourite *Cold Feet* scene because a lot of people – punters and the like – actually believe that I smacked him for real. When I saw it at a preview, I was shocked myself. Although the angle from which it was filmed makes it look nearer than it was, it was still fairly close – there was a definite whistle. The hard thing was to try and make it all look naturalistic. I didn't know the layout of the desks, so I couldn't just storm across them. There's one bit where I fall clumsily and it was difficult to fall and make it look real. There's another bit where one of the extras decided to improvise and shouted at me: "What are you doing?" I shouted back: "Shut up!" The motivation for me saying "Shut up" was that he wasn't actually meant to be saying anything! Actually, he did me a favour because it fitted in quite well.'

SCENE 61 INT
SET ADAM'S OFFICE
DAY 3 1425

ADAM:
PETE:
RECEPTIONIST OOV:
Office Workers:

ADAM IS SITTING AT HIS DESK IN THE
OPEN PLAN OFFICE, WORKING AT HIS
COMPUTER SCREEN, WHEN HIS PHONE
RINGS. HE SNATCHES IT UP.

      ADAM:

Adam Williams.

      RECEPTIONIST OOV:

This is reception. We've a Pete

Gifford to see you.

      ADAM:

(SURPRISED) PETE? (SHRUGS) Oh,

well, send him through, will you.

ADAM REPLACES THE PHONE AND BRIEFLY
TYPES SOMETHING ELSE ON HIS SCREEN
WHILE HE WAITS FOR PETE TO COME
THROUGH FROM RECEPTION. THE DOOR
AT THE FAR END OF THE OFFICE DULY
OPENS AND PETE APPEARS. HE STANDS
LOOKING AROUND FOR ADAM'S DESK.
ADAM WAVES HIM OVER. PETE STRIDES
THROUGH THE OPEN PLAN OFFICE AND
SOME DISTANCE FROM ADAM STARTS
SHOUTING AT HIM. HEADS TURN TO SEE
WHAT THE COMMOTION'S ABOUT.

      PETE:

(SHOUTS) You shit! To think I

trusted you. I should have guessed

from her description. Especially

the arrogant bit. And when she

tells you, what do you do? Take

advantage. While I'm listening in

on the phone!

PETE ARRIVES AT ADAM'S DESK. NOW EVERYONE IN THE OFFICE IS WATCHING. ADAM STARES AT PETE DUMBSTRUCK. PETE EYES HIM COLDLY.

PETE:

(WITH CONTROLLED VENOM) You shit!

PETE UNLEASHES A RIGHT HOOK, WHICH SENDS ADAM SPRAWLING ON THE FLOOR BELOW HIS DESK. SECRETARIES GASP. PETE STANDS OVER ADAM.

PETE:

You don't see her. You don't talk

to her. You stay away!

WITHOUT WAITING FOR A REPLY, PETE TURNS ON HIS HEEL AND STRIDES OUT OF THE OFFICE; NO ONE CHALLENGES HIM. ADAM PULLS HIMSELF TO HIS FEET AND GINGERLY FEELS HIS EYE.

ADAM:

(TO THE OFFICE) It's okay. He's a

friend of mine.

PEOPLE GO BACK TO WORK. ADAM STARES AT THE DOORS, NOW SWINGING SHUT AFTER PETE'S BURST THROUGH THEM, AND WONDERS WHAT THE HELL ALL THAT WAS ABOUT.

CUT TO SCENE 62 INT ADAM'S UPSTAIRS LANDING/SPARE ROOM

END OF PART TWO

155

Jacey Salles (Ramona):

'The scenes I like best as Ramona are the ones which show the tension with David because otherwise I'm just doing household chores. I think every scene I had in the first series was with children. Some days they co-operate and want to do it; other times they just get bored like we do sometimes. I try to get to know them between takes and coax them into doing things, but if they're in that kind of mood there's nothing you can do with two-year-olds. I remember there was a scene where I was meant to chase Josh around with a potty to the accompaniment of wild Spanish music. That took so long to do because the child wouldn't come to me, nor would he go away from me. It seemed static, and so I was amazed when it was cut that there was so much movement. I was wearing skin-tight trousers so I couldn't even bend down, but they had me crawling in between chairs and everything. It took nearly an hour to do and was really exhausting. At the end, I just sighed, "Oooh", thinking how much more can I do? And they actually kept that in as Ramona's reaction.

'Ramona comes from Barcelona and is very excitable. The brief when I got the part was that she is supposed to be the complete antithesis to David and Karen. So whereas they're very British, quiet and reserved, and keep their emotions in, Ramona is meant to be just the opposite. David can't cope with Ramona being so honest, open, loud and emotional. He finds it hard, sharing his living space with her, whereas Karen finds it fun and refreshing. In a perverse way, Karen quite enjoys the tension that is created because it makes David uncomfortable. Ramona thinks Karen is so cool, relaxed and chilled out, but she sees David as so uptight – a wet blanket with not an ounce of passion in him.

'Ramona is not thick, but she feels frustrated sometimes that David either treats her like an idiot or talks so quickly that it makes her look like an idiot. Either way, he's not very helpful to Ramona. He's always muttering under his breath. She's aware that he's doing that and she wishes she had the language to deal with him. Her English has improved from being very pidgin and she understands a lot more than she used to, but he still uses his position and the language over her. So it becomes this battle of wills between them.

'One scene which illustrates this nicely is after he has lost his job. He decides he is going to stay at home and look after Josh and, as part of the cutbacks, he suggests sacking the nanny. Ramona overhears this and thinks "Ha! Right, so you don't need me!" She then goes on a work-to-rule and refuses to answer the door, etc. Then David gets in a mess over dinner and burns everything. Suddenly, he's in her environment and he needs her help. She enjoys his discomfiture and he has to bribe her £30 into doing the cooking.'

The Scripts

SCENE 76 INT
SET   DAVID & KAREN'S KITCHEN
NIGHT 4 1930

DAVID:
RAMONA:
KAREN:
NATALIE:
GEORGE:

DAVID, STILL IN HIS APRON, A PAIR
OF OVEN GLOVES ON, HIS HAIR MUSSED
WITH FLOUR, IS LOOKING DEEPLY
ANXIOUS - CLEARLY COOKING IS NOT AS
EASY AS JUST FOLLOWING
INSTRUCTIONS. (WE CAN'T SEE THE
WHOLE KITCHEN). THE DOORBELL IS
RUNG. DAVID LOOKS TOWARDS THE
FRONT DOOR THEN BACK, MAKING NO
EFFORT TO ANSWER IT. FROM UPSTAIRS
COMES KAREN'S VOICE.

                KAREN: OOV

David! Can you get that?

DAVID ROLLS HIS EYES AS HE GOES TO
THE DOOR.

DAVID:

(MUTTERING) "Yes sir, yes sir,

three bags full."

DAVID REMOVES THE OVEN GLOVES FROM
ONE HAND AND OPENS THE DOOR.
STANDING ON THE THRESHOLD IS
NATALIE AND HER HUSBAND. DAVID IS
CONSIDERABLY TAKEN ABACK.

DAVID:

Natalie! What are you doing here?

NATALIE:

(ENTERING) Well, I thought I'd

been invited to dinner. You

haven't met my new husband, have

you? George, this is David.

DAVID MUTTERS AS HE SHAKES GEORGE'S
HAND. KAREN APPEARS ON THE STAIRS.

KAREN:

Natalie! So glad you could make

it. (TO DAVID) Natalie's a member

of that health club I never go to.

DAVID:

(SMILES WEAKLY; TO NATALIE AND

GEORGE) Really? Excuse me, I must

just, erm... the kitchen.

DAVID FLEES.

CUT TO SCENE 77 INT DAVID & KAREN'S
KITCHEN

SCENE 77 INT
SET DAVID & KAREN'S KITCHEN
NIGHT 4 1932

DAVID:
RAMONA:

DAVID CLOSES THE KITCHEN DOOR AND
LEANS AGAINST IT, WONDERING WHAT
THE HELL NATALIE IS DOING HERE. HE
LOOKS UP... AT RAMONA WHO'S TRYING
TO SAVE THE MEAL.

      DAVID:

Well, what do you think?

      RAMONA:

(PULLS A FACE)   David, I don't

know.

      DAVID:

Alright, I'll make it thirty pounds!

      RAMONA:

(WEIGHING UP THIS OFFER)   Okay!

RAMONA THROWS SOME SPICES INTO A
SAUCEPAN AND ASSUMES CONTROL OF THE
COOKING. DAVID LOOKS RELIEVED -
SAVED!

CUT TO SCENE 78 INT BAR

Director Tom Vaughan:

'In episode three, we had Pete and Amy going on one of those company activity courses, doing things like paintballing and canoeing. They're supposed to be good for bonding and for picking out natural leaders. Pete and Amy are just beginning to get friendly in this episode. He has been comforting her after her split from Adam and they end up getting lost on the course in the pouring rain and spending the night in a hotel together. We did the exercise scenes at Tatton Park outside Manchester. We treated the paintballing scene like a bad action movie and I know John had great fun doing it. We had paintball experts on hand to advise us because you have to be careful with those guns. They can be dangerous – they do hurt. In fact, Rosie Cavaliero, the actress playing Amy, was hit on the chest – which wasn't where she was supposed to be hit at all – and it was a bit painful for a few minutes. But she was soon OK.

'John wasn't quite as keen on doing the scene where he had to end up in the water while canoeing. The water that day was freezing, but he decided he wanted to do it first thing in the morning so he could dry out.'

John Thomson (Pete):

'During the paintballing, I shot one of the extras in the hand and it kills – it really, really hurts. I felt terrible about it. These things you shoot are so powerful they break the skin. You need medical attention. Then out of the blue I got shot on the hand, too – it was like being strapped at school. We wore body protection, but the guys who run the place said that if you get hit on the forehead it comes up like a golf ball. I remember one guy got hit in the throat. Fortunately, it was from long distance but he emitted this feminine cry and turned to the paintballer and said: "Do you know what you're bloody doing?" One thing that gutted me was I thought we were going to be able to have a go for real afterwards, but we didn't have time. I'd never done it before, but I'm a dab hand with a gun at clay pigeon shooting.

'As for the canoeing stuff, I wasn't actually chucked in the water because there were leeches. So I was just soaked by having buckets of water thrown over me. I do all my own stunts ...'

SCENE   53 EXT
SET   WOODS
DAY 10 1254

AMY:
PETE:
Other Participants:

A PAINTBALL GAME IS IN PROGRESS
BETWEEN TWO TEAMS WEARING COMBAT
FATIGUES AND PROTECTIVE HEADGEAR
AND SPORTING DIFFERENT COLOURED
RIBBONS TO SHOW WHICH SIDE THEY'RE
ON. A FIGURE (AMY) HIDES BEHIND A
TREE. ANOTHER PERSON ON THE SAME
TEAM (PETE) COMES RACING UP TO JOIN
HER.

   AMY:

We're being outflanked on the right

   PETE:

Who cares?! What time's lunch?

SUDDENLY AN ATTACKER FROM THE
OPPOSING TEAM POPS UP YARD IN FRONT
OF AMY, PREPARING TO SHOOT HER.

   PETE:

Amy!!

         PETE SHOOTS THE GUY WITH PAINT,
         JUST BEFORE HE CAN GET HIS SHOT OFF
         AT AMY. THE BLOKE RAISES HIS HAND
         TO INDICATE HE'S OUT OF THE GAME.
         THE BATTLE IS MOMENTARILY FORGOTTEN
         AS AMY TURNS TO PETE.

            AMY:

         You saved my life.

         THROUGH THEIR PROTECTIVE HEADGEAR,
         THEY SHARE A MEANINGFUL MOMENT.
         TILL ANOTHER ATTACKER POPS UP YARDS
         FROM PETE AND WITH A BLOOD-CURDLING
         SCREAM, SHOOTS HIM IN THE CHEST.
         SOMEONE ELSE SHOOTS THIS GUY. AMY
         LOOKS AT PETE - "OH".

         CUT SCENE 54 INT TRAIN

SCENE 64 INT
SET   TRAVELODGE
NIGHT 10 2055

PETE:
AMY:
RECEPTIONIST:

PETE, IN HIS PINK TRACKSUIT, AND
AMY, BOTH LOOKING LIKE DROWNED
RATS, STAND AT RECEPTION AS THE
RECEPTIONIST CHECKS HIS COMPUTER.

            AMY:

(ASIDE TO PETE) I've only got a

tenner on me.

PETE PULLS A CREDIT CARD OUT OF HIS
POCKET AND HOLDS IT UP TRIUMPHANTLY

            PETE:

I used to be a scout. Briefly.

THE RECEPTIONIST LOOKS UP FROM HIS
COMPUTER.

            RECEPTIONIST:

And will you be requiring one room

or two?

                        PETE:

                  Two please.

                  ANY STOPS THE RECEPTIONIST WITH A
                  LOOK THEN PUTS HER HAND ON PETE'S
                  ARM.

                              AMY:

                  (TO PETE) We could just have one.

                  If you like.

                  PETE LOOKS AT AMY, THEN AT THE
                  RECEPTIONIST, WONDERING WHAT HE
                  SHOULD DO. THE RECEPTIONIST
                  REGARDS HIM QUIZZICALLY - "IT'S
                  YOUR CALL".

                  CUT TO SCENE 65 INT RESTAURANT

Writer Mike Bullen:

'Christine and I had a nice idea for a storyline that David and Karen, in trying to surprise each other for their anniversary, would both cock it up. They would unknowingly be going off in different directions and the ending to the episode would be seeing them going their separate ways and knowing that they weren't going to meet up. When Andy read the script, he said: "This story has no ending." We said that was the point, to leave it open-ended. So we shouted him down. But as the programme was being cut together, the editor said: "This story has no ending." Now when it's just one person's opinion you can ague, but when others start saying the same thing, you'd better sit up and take notice. Clearly Andy had been right – we lacked an ending.

'So someone suggested that David and Karen should go to Paris. It was a bit of a nightmare for me because as the writer it's very difficult to write scenes afterwards when you have done all you want to do. To be told to tack on another bit is not as easy as it sounds. But they managed to have a one-day shoot in Paris and give it a nice romantic ending. And I have to say it is much, much better than what was there originally. As a writer, I think I have the clearest vision of what *Cold Feet* is about and yet I'm quite often wrong and have to be aware that others have valid contributions. Sometimes I have to lose a funny line because one of the cast or someone in the office will query whether it is true to character. But that's fair enough because the cast know their characters inside out. And whilst they may occasionally ask whether a line can be changed, or at least delivered in a different way, they are very trusting regarding the actual storylines.'

Director Tom Vaughan:

'In the original script David and Karen were going to be left going their separate ways on a plane and a train, but we felt we needed a pay-off for these two because the other characters all have dramatic endings in this episode. Pete and Amy finish up spending the night in a hotel room, while Adam's blind date leads to an awkward encounter with Rachel and her new young boyfriend Danny at a Chinese restaurant. They are both fairly "down" endings so we felt that, in order to balance it out, we needed an uplifting moment where Karen somehow gets to Paris to meet up with David on their wedding anniversary.

'There was a two-day break before the end of filming that episode and we put our heads together to think of what we could do to shoot a finale. We decided to hire a minimum French crew and go filming in Paris for the night. So Christine Langan, director of photography Peter Middleton, Robert Bathurst and I caught the train to Paris and arranged to meet Hermione Norris at the Eiffel Tower at sunset. We met Hermione as planned and just set off from there. Mike Bullen had written a scene where David is having a go at Natalie over the phone, but the rest we just improvised as we went along.

'We found a little restaurant with Notre Dame in the background and said: "Can we film here?" The owner said yes, so off we went. It was exciting, just winging it like that, but also nerve-racking, especially when, while we were still filming, our beautifully illuminated backdrop suddenly went dark. Unbeknown to us, they turn the lights off at Notre Dame at midnight. So we got the crew to turn on their car headlights and shine them across the Seine to light up Notre Dame again. Somehow we managed to get away with it all and even got the Eiffel Tower in shot as a bonus. But it was pretty hair-raising stuff.'

Hermione Norris (Karen):

'Paris was a real bonus and suddenly finding ourselves there rather than Manchester was rather appealing. We met at the Eiffel Tower just as the sun was setting and it was quite magical. Robert and I were walking around the grounds shell-shocked – it was quite surreal. Unfortunately, French crews have long meal breaks, which was why the lights on Notre Dame went off before we had finished, but Pete Middleton's brainwave of pointing all our car headlights at the building worked a treat. The other reason I particularly like that scene is that it shows the love and tenderness between Karen and David after all the sniping that had been going on.'

Director Tom Vaughan:

'A scene I particularly like is the dinner-party sequence where Karen splits in two as she smokes a spliff. She is undergoing a life crisis and tries to be rebellious and not only is the scene a really good start to the episode in terms of setting up the characters, but it also has a dig at middle-class dinner parties in general. And there is a great supporting cast around the dinner table – characters who we don't normally see, but who are part of David and Karen's middle-class world. I love the way that opera is playing in the background while Karen smokes the joint, and then when she looks up she sees herself.

'We see the two sides of Karen – the calm, sensible one and the aggressive one. We did two separate passes of Hermione – one of her standing and talking to an empty space at the table; the other of her sitting at the table and looking up at nobody. By editing them together, we made it seem as if there were two Karens in the room. For shots over the shoulder of one "Karen" looking towards the other, we used an identically-dressed double in a blonde wig. In fact, Hermione's double was so convincing that even the crew got confused at times! Obviously, every viewer knows it's a special effect, but it was still fun to do. It's nice to be able to do something a bit different like a fantasy scene.

'It's funny but a scene like that, which is potentially complicated, often causes fewer headaches than something relatively straightforward. In the same episode, there is a scene where Karen has a tattoo of a gecko done on her bottom. Again, it's part of her new image. We found a tattoo parlour in Manchester, but the owner said he would only let us film there if we promised we weren't going to give tattooing a bad name, which we weren't. But when we turned up to start filming, the owner took one look at our actor playing the tattooist, saw that he was covered in tattoos and jumped to the conclusion that we'd be taking the mickey. So he wouldn't let us film. This went on for an hour. Eventually, after lengthy negotiations, he relented and we were finally able to get on with shooting the scene.'

Hermione Norris (Karen):

'The dinner party scene is extremely observant, showing how Karen's life has changed and how people get into that really staid, dull routine of having to invite people you don't like round to dinner on a regular basis. It shows her waking up to find herself living this life that she didn't want, or expect, to be living – this life that she's bought into. I thought it was really well written.'

The Scripts

```
SCENE  8 INT
SET  DAVID & KAREN'S LOUNGE
NIGHT 1 2140

KAREN:

KAREN STANDS, THE PHONE TO HER EAR.
THE CHATTER AND LAUGHTER OF THE
DINNER PARTY CAN BE HEARD COMING
FROM THE OTHER ROOM.

          KAREN:

Help!!!

CUT TO SCENE 9 INT BAR
```

THIS SCENE WILL NEED TO BE SPLIT
BETWEEN INT BAR & INT DAVID & KAREN'S
LOUNGE - IT WILL BE TWO PART SCENES.

<u>SCENE 9 INT</u>
<u>SET BAR</u>
<u>NIGHT 1</u> 2140

RACHEL:
DANNY:
STU:
BECCA:
ZAC:
Other Extras:

RACHEL HUGS HER MOBILE PHONE TO HER
EAR, STRAINING TO HEAR THE
CONVERSATION OVER THE NOISE OF A
LOUD AND LIVELY BAR. SHE HAS TO
SHOUT TO MAKE HERSELF HEARD. SHE'S
WITH DANNY AND SOME OF HIS FRIENDS
(STU, BECCA AND ZAC, ALL THE SAME
AGE AS HIM).

       RACHEL:

(AMUSED) What's the matter?

INTERCUT BETWEEN KAREN AND RACHEL.

AMENDED 23.4.99

            KAREN:

I've died and gone to hell. Or

worse I'm still here and this is my

life. Where are you?

            RACHEL:

Bar Nexus.

            KAREN:

Can I come?

            RACHEL:

I thought you were having a dinner

party.

            KAREN:

We are. I'm not sure I can stand

it.

            RACHEL:

Well you know the best way to

handle it.

            KAREN:

I'm already pissed.

            RACHEL:

Then roll a joint.

            KAREN:

(HALF SERIOUSLY) I would if I had

any dope.

A BEAT.

            RACHEL:

You might find a stray spliff in my

bedside table. Second drawer down.

AMENDED. 20.4.99
            KAREN:

Rachel! (BEAT) Second drawer

down did you say?

CUT TO SCENE 10 INT DAVID & KAREN'S
DINING ROOM

SCENE 10 INT
SET DAVID & KAREN'S DINING ROOM
NIGHT 1 2145

DAVID:
KAREN:
NATASHA:
MARK:
LAURA:
JAMES:

THE DINNER PARTY HAS REACHED COFFEE
STAGE. EACH OF THE PARTICIPANTS
ALSO HAS A LIQUEUR. DAVID AND MARK
PUFF CIGARS. AS BEFORE,
CONVERSATION IS LIVELY.

                NATASHA:

I love auctions! And there's always

the chance you'll find a bargain.

Last week I stumbled on a painting.

I think it might be by the Norwich

School.

JAMES:

(TEASING HER)   It's of a Norwich
School.

THE MEN CHORTLE. LAURA TURNS TO
KAREN FOR SUPPORT.

NATASHA:

Karen, you studied art history...

ALL EYES TURN TO KAREN AND ARE
RATHER ASTONISHED TO FIND HER IN THE
LATTER STAGES OF MAKING A HUGE
JOINT. SHE'S JUST ATTEMPTING TO
LIGHT IT, PUFFING IN AS SHE HOLDS A
MATCH TO THE END. JUST AS SHE TAKES
HER FIRST DEEP TOKE, SHE CATCHES
THEM ALL STARING AT HER. SHE
PRESUMES THEY'RE WAITING TO BE
OFFERED SOME.

KAREN:

(HOLDING JOINT OUT)   Sorry? Would

you like some?

DAVID IS SPEECHLESS. JAMES, NATASHA
AND LAURA MAKE APOLOGETIC NOISES.
MARK SAYS NOTHING.

JAMES/**NATASHA**/LAURA (SIMULTANEOUSLY)

I don't, thanks. (JAMES)
Now that we've got kids. (NATASHA)
I've got to be up early... (LAURA)

KAREN SHRUGS - SUIT YOURSELVES AND
PUFFS CONTENTEDLY ON HER SPLIFF.
THE OTHERS JUST WATCH.

CUT TO SCENE 11 INT KAREN & DAVID'S
BATHROOM

SCENE 11 INT
SET DAVID & KAREN'S BATHROOM
NIGHT 1 2310

DAVID:
KAREN:

DAVID AND KAREN ARE GETTING READY
FOR BED. DAVID IS EXTREMELY WORKED
UP, AGITATEDLY STRIDING AS KAREN
BRUSHES HER TEETH.

DAVID:

Were you out of your mind?!!

KAREN:

Briefly. I don't think it was
particularly good stuff.

DAVID:

I have never been so embarrassed!

KAREN:

Oh, come on, David! ("HAVE YOU
FORGOTTEN?") School nativity play?
One of the three wise men wet
himself? (OFF DAVID'S ASTONISHED
STARE - "HOW DO YOU KNOW ABOUT
THAT?!") Your mother told me.

DAVID:

You do not offer marijuana at dinner
parties!

KAREN:

You offered Cuban cigars. Which
smell a lot worse.

DAVID:

Yes, but they're not illegal.

KAREN:

In America they are. (OFF DAVID'S
NON FORGIVING LOOK) I was bored,
David. Bored rigid.

DAVID:

You were certainly quiet. Perhaps
if you'd got more involved...

KAREN:

(UNAPOLOGETICALLY) I'm sorry. I
had no interest in discussing
nannies. Again.

DAVID:

That wasn't all we talked about.

KAREN:

Or skiing holidays, house prices or

private education.

DAVID:

Well, you could have started a

conversation of your own.

KAREN:

I tried.

DAVID:

(REMEMBERIN, FLATLY) Oh, yes.

CUT TO SCENE 12 INT DAVID & KAREN'S
DINING ROOM

SCENE 12 INT
SET DAVID & KAREN'S DINING ROOM
NIGHT 1 (FLASHBACK) 2118

KAREN:
JAMES:
DAVID:
NATASHA:
MARK:
LAURA:

EARLIER IN THE EVENING. KAREN IS
DISHING OUT THE DESSERTS WHICH ARE
THEN BEING PASSED ALONG THE TABLE.
JAMES IS IN MID-CONVERSATION.

JAMES:

After I go to New York next week I

should have enough frequent flyer

miles for two free trips to south

east Asia.

GENERAL MURMURS OF APPROVAL,
ENVY,ETC.

AMENDED 20.4.99
                    KAREN:

Did you know that there's a tribe in

Borneo where instead of shaking

hands on a deal, men masturbate one

another?

SILENCE. NOBODY QUITE KNOWS HOW TO
REACT TO THIS TITBIT OF INFORMATION.

                    NATASHA:

(TO LAURA) Have you decided where

you're going on holiday this year?

CUT BACK TO SCENE 13 INT DAVID &
KAREN'S **BATHROOM**

SCENE 13 INT
SET DAVID & KAREN'S **BATHROOM**
NIGHT 1 2312

DAVID:
KAREN:

DAVID AND KAREN AS BEFORE. DAVID
IS NOW BRUSHING HIS TEETH AS KAREN
REMOVES HER MAKE-UP.

                    DAVID:

They'll never invite us back.

                    KAREN:

Well, hooray. We won't have to

admire their antiques.

                    DAVID:

I don't know what's got into you!

These are our friends.

                    KAREN:

(GLOOMILY) I know.

AMENDED 20.4.99

DAVID:

I'm never going to be able to get to

sleep!

KAREN:

(HE'S SUCH A BABY) You would if

you'd only relax.

DAVID:

(SARCASTICALLY) Oh, and how do you

suggest I do that?

**FROM THE POCKET OF HER DRESSING
GOWN, KAREN REMOVES THE DOG-END OF
THE JOINT SHE WAS SMOKING EARLIER.**

KAREN:

(HOLDING UP DOG-END) I didn't
finish it.

**LOOKING UTTERLY DISAPPROVING, DAVID
SNATCHES THE DOG-END FROM KAREN'S
FINGERS AND FLUSHES IT DOWN THE LOO
- "THERE!". KAREN SIMPLY GRINS,
AMUSED AT HIS UP-TIGHTEDNESS.**

CUT TO SCENE 14 INT PETE & JENNY'S
BEDROOM

Writer Mike Bullen:

'We pride ourselves on the fact that *Cold Feet* is something that people recognize and is true to the lives of the age we are reflecting. It is very important to me that we do that. We ran into problems in episode four of series two, where Karen, bored with her life, smokes the joint at the dinner party and later on, has another joint with Adam at the school reunion. We had to send the script to a department called Compliance and they check that you are not libelling anyone. They also check that scripts adhere to the ITC code of conduct. Our script fell foul because apparently you can only show drug usage if it is shown to have some cost to the people involved. It can't be completely risk-free or guilt-free. It has to be seen to be an anti-social activity – you have to portray it in a bad light. Their suggestion was that when Karen and Adam were smoking the joint at the school reunion, the police could burst in and arrest them. Firstly, I said it was ludicrous and secondly, we had already done that with ecstasy in series one. So I was very unhappy about it. The compromise was that I had to write an extra scene in which we had an anti-drugs message. I am not an advocate of drug usage, but I do think we should be allowed, as grown-ups making a post-watershed programme, to show life as it is, which to me means there are people who smoke joints without feeling the world is about to end.

'So to get around the rules I decided to put the anti-drugs message into the most buffoonish of characters. So it is David who catches Ramona coming downstairs with a dog-end of a roll-your-own. And he starts lecturing her on how it's a slippery slope, how one minute you're smoking marijuana and the next, you're bashing old ladies over the head to feed your drug habit. The punch at the end is that when he discovers it's only tobacco, he says: "Oh, it's harmless then." Ramona comes back with: "No, it's tobacco. It causes cancer." That to me seems to be more of an issue than what the ITC were insisting.

'So I quite enjoy the scene because you could have lifted it out and the episode would not have been damaged. That was why I didn't want to write it – you don't always want to write scenes that don't have to be there. But given that I had to write it, I was quite pleased with the way I managed to subvert the message.'

Robert Bathurst (David):

'I was the voice of the Independent Television Commission here. I was aware when I did it that the anti-drugs message had been given to the most priggish character on the show, which rather undermined the message. It was like one of those financial disclaimers. But I thought it was a neat device and worked rather well. It's strange that things get queried in comedies which don't in dramas. In comedy, sex and drugs are seen as distasteful, yet in drama they're mandatory.

'I would say that David's attitude to his nanny is fairly consistent. The only time he's been nice to her was on Lindisfarne and that scene was cut. He did a touching toast to Ramona at the end of dinner – the only time he's ever looked her in the eye. He did once try to jump into bed with her, of course, but that was purely a misunderstanding and anyway, he never looked her in the eye because when he turned round, he found that in fact he was looking into the eyes of his wife!'

Jacey Salles (Ramona):

'This is a good scene because for once Ramona has the last word. It shows how she is starting to assert herself as she learns the language a bit more. She is more confident and established in the house and isn't going to be picked on by David. It shows that in a one-on-one she can come out on top. She can give as good as she gets. We know that David doesn't like smoking, but Karen has told Ramona she can smoke. And, much to David's annoyance, Ramona always takes her orders from Karen.'

SCENE 69A INT
SET DAVID & KAREN'S KITCHEN/
HALL
NIGHT 8

DAVID:
RAMONA:

DAVID CLOSES THE FRONT DOOR BEHIND
HIM, CARRYING HIS SPORTS BAG AS HE
RETURNS FROM HIS GAME OF SQUASH
WITH ADAM; HE'S SMOKING A SMALL
CIGAR. AS HE ENTERS, RAMONA COMES
DOWN THE STAIRS CARRYING AN
ASH-TRAY WITH DOG END IN IT. DAVID
NOTICES THIS, AND HIS FACE
REGISTERS SHOCKED DISAPPROVAL. HE
GOES HARING AFTER RAMONA INTO THE
KITCHEN, AND TAKING THE CIGAR FROM
HIS MOUTH, GRABS THE ASHTRAY OUT OF
HER HAND BEFORE SHE CAN DISPOSE OF
ITS CONTENTS IN THE BIN.

          DAVID:

Ramona! What are you doing?!

          RAMONA:

Tidying up, you let me.

                          151B 4
     AMENDED 16.5.99

          DAVID:

(HOLDING UP DOG-END; ACCUSINGLY)

Is this yours?

          RAMONA:

(GUILTILY) Is Javier's. (QUICKLY)
Karen say is okay in my room.

          DAVID:

(EYES WIDENING; HE CAN'T BELIEVE

KAREN'S DECLINING MORAL STANDARDS)

My God, this house is becoming a

crack den!

RAMONA STARES AT HIM IN CONFUSION -
WHAT'S HE ON ABOUT?

DAVID:

Karen knows my attitude towards drugs.

RAMONA:

Drugs?!

DAVID:

I will not tolerate them in this house.

RAMONA:

Is not drugs!

DAVID:

I mean, where does it end? It starts with marijuana, before you know it, you're robbing old ladies to pay for cocaine.

AMENDED 16.5.99
RAMONA:

David, is no marijuana!

DAVID:

(LEAPING ON THIS) You see!! Already you're lying to hide your addiction! It's a slippery slope Ramona!

RAMONA:

(ANGRILY) David, I no lie! I no

take drugs! I good Catholic girl.

(BEAT; SHRUGS) Well, I Catholic

girls. (SNATCHES DOG-END FROM HIM

AND BRANDISHES IT IN HIS FACE) This

no drugs! Is cigarette.

DAVID IS STOPPED IN HIS TRACKS BY
THIS CONTENTION. A BEAT.

DAVID:

(UNCERTAINLY) It's not pot? Karen

didn't give it to you?

RAMONA:

Karen say she no do it again. It

give her headache. No, David, is

tobacco. Javier he roll up his own.

DAVID BREAKS INTO A SAMILE, AMUSED
BY HIS OWN PARANOIA. RELAXING HE
STARTS SMOKING HIS CIGAR AGAIN.

DAVID:

(WITH RELIEF) You mean, it's

harmless?

AMENDED 16.5.99
RAMONA:

("WEREN'T YOU LISTENING?!") No!

Is tobacco! (TAKES DAVID'S CIGAR

FROM HIS MOUTH AND STUBS IT OUT IN

THE ASHTRAY) He give you cancer!

RAMONA ROUGHLY SHOVES THE ASHTRAY
TOWARDS DAVID, FORCING HIM TO TAKE
IT, THEN TURNS ON HER HEELS AND
MARCHES OUT OF THE ROOM, LEAVING
DAVID LOOKING SHOCKED AT BEING
SPOKEN TO IN THAT WAY. HE LOOKS
DOWN AT HIS CIGAR, WHICH LIES IN
THE ASHTRAY CRUSHED, NOT DISSIMILAR
TO HOW DAVID'S FEELING RIGHT AT
THIS MOMENT.

CUT TO SC 70 EXT CENTRAL MANCHESTER

Director Pete Travis:

'A scene which I really like is the one where Jenny tells Pete that he has to move out. It's very sad, but at the same time very funny and is a tribute, not only to Mike Bullen's great writing, but also to two wonderful performances from Fay Ripley and John Thomson. The scene is particularly important in the overall story of *Cold Feet* because it shows that time when the relationship between Pete and Jenny – which is probably the one which the audience cares about most – falls apart.

'To make it look as realistic as possible and to give it a documentary-style feel, I shot it all with a hand-held camera. That lovely shot where you see Pete dragging his case along the corridor by the strap, that was John's idea. And it was John who came up with the suggestion that Pete should have to put all his worldly possessions into plastic bags. It made his plight seem all the more miserable. As I say, Fay was brilliant in that scene and I was able to go through to the finish without a cut. After Adam and Pete had gone, she cried her tears on cue and then did that fabulous bit right at the end of kicking the table in despair.'

Fay Ripley (Jenny):

'I love working with John Thomson because there's no chance of you taking yourself too seriously. He's a very funny man and we like to play. In the scene where Jenny threw Pete out, John was finding himself very amusing with his bag on wheels, while I was trying to do my method acting with tears in the corner. John would just come on and crack up, wheeling his trolley behind him. I'm afraid we do "corpse" rather a lot.

'The scene in episode two where we visualize each other as slobs was fun to do, too. John was eating spaghetti, with it dribbling down his chin. I think we had a sick bucket on standby for John that day because he may have been mildly hungover and the cold spaghetti wasn't going down that well. For my part, I had to swig and then spit out some beer in my Italian whore's outfit. I enjoyed that, partly because I got to wear a corset but also because I got to spit beer all over John. That scene needed quite a few takes, too – funny that!

'Jenny's very ballsy and speaks her mind, but she's more sensitive than people give her credit for. She's seen as very hard but I don't think she is – it's just that she won't

Cold Feet – the best bits...

show her vulnerability to everyone. She'll always stick up for the underdog.

'Robert Bathurst's character, David, makes me crack up. There's a great scene – really short – where David's in a phone box and an old woman is waiting outside. You can't hear him speaking but he tells her he'll only be two minutes by holding up two fingers. She thinks he's telling her to pee off. I don't know why, but that always makes me laugh. Jokes against old people never fail! David and Jenny are quite unpopular with the public. Women come up to me in the street and say: "How dare you treat poor Pete like that!" I say, "Excuse me, he had an affair." "So did you," they say, whereupon I point out that mine was purely fantasy. And they tell Robert: "Oh, you are a pig to your lovely wife!" So Robert and I are comrades. We stick together in case we get tomatoes thrown at us in the street.'

Writer Mike Bullen:

'People said to me at the end of series one that they didn't think David and Karen's relationship would last, but that Pete and Jen were such a strong couple. So that made me decide in series two that I would split Pete and Jen up and have David and Karen getting stronger, because I think life is like that. When you go to a wedding, everyone has a view on how good the couple getting married are – how long it will last. But people don't know – nobody knows how things will turn out. I thought there were interesting things to do with those characters in terms of splitting them up – it's an area we hadn't really done before – and besides, it's quite common for people of that age to separate. The other attraction was that, with Adam and Rachel happily together at the end of series two, I needed a contrast. It didn't offer me much mileage to have three happy couples.'

SCENE 4 INT
SET PETE & JENNY'S LOUNGE
DAY 1 1830

JENNY:
ADAM:
PETE:
BABY ADAM:

JENNY HOLDS BABY ADAM; ADAM STANDS
UNCOMFORTABLY.

ADAM:

You know, you'd find it much easier

to talk this through if he was

still living here.

JENNY:

Maybe that's why I'm kicking him

out.

ADAM SIGHS; JENNY'S NOT TO BE
SPOKEN TO WHEN SHE'S IN THIS SORT
OF A MOOD.

ADAM:

He's stopped seeing her, you know.

JENNY:

They work together!

ADAM:

Yeah, I know, but...

JENNY:

(INTERRUPTING; BROOKING NO FURTHER

DISCUSSION) Adam!

ADAM FALLS SILENT. PETE WANDERS
PAST THE OPEN DOOR, DRAGGING A
LARGE SUITCASE.

JENNY:

(TO PETE) Oi, oi, oi!!! Where do

you think you are going with that?

PETE STOPS AND LOOKS IN.

PETE:

Adam's.

JENNY:

No, you're not.

PETE STEALS A LOOK AT ADAM, HOPING
THAT HIS DIPLOMACY HAS PAID OFF.

PETE:

You mean, I can stay?

JENNY:

I mean you're not taking that

suitcase. We bought that together.

My half stays here.

PETE:

What am I supposed to cart my gear

in, then?

JENNY:

There are some plastic bags under

the sink. You can have five.

FORLORNLY, PETE DRAGS THE SUITCASE
OFF TOWARDS THE KITCHEN.

ADAM:

(TO JEN) Aren't you maybe being a

bit hard on him?

A BEAT.

JENNY:

(DOUBT CREEPING INTO HER VOICE) Do

you think so?

ADAM NODS. ANOTHER BEAT.

JENNY:

(CALLING SO PETE CAN HEAR) All

right. You can have six!

JENNY LOOKS DEFIANTLY AT ADAM - "IS
THAT BETTER?"

ADAM:

So what, that's it? Your marriage

is over?

JENNY:

I gave him a chance. He didn't

stop seeing her.

ADAM:

Yeah, but he didn't *know* you were

giving him a chance. It was *me*

that gave him the ultimatum. It

was me he gave his word to. So you

could argue it was me he betrayed.

JENNY COUGHS - "EXCUSE ME?!"

ADAM:

Okay, maybe I could have put that

better. Look, just don't kick him

out.

If for no other reason than I don't

want to live with him. Not while

he's as miserable as he is anyway.

JENNY:

My heart bleeds.

PETE REAPPEARS IN THE DOORWAY,
CLUTCHING SIX PLASTIC BAGS STUFFED
WITH CLOTHES.

PETE:

(MISERABLY) I'm ready then.

JENNY:

You got a picture of your son?

PETE:

(REALISING HE HASN'T) Oh.

JENNY ROLLS HER EYES. SHE HANDS
BABY ADAM TO PETE AND CROSSES TO A
BUREAU TO FIND PETE A PHOTO.

JENNY:

Who's going to look after you now I

won't?

PETE LOOKS AT ADAM. ADAM CATCHES
THE GLANCE AND REALISES THE TORCH
IS BEING PASSED TO HIM. HE TURNS
TO JENNY.

ADAM:

(TO JENNY, BESEECHINGLY) Please,

Jen!

JENNY BRINGS A PHOTO OF PETE.

JENNY:

Here. You can have this one. It's

old; we're smiling.

PETE TAKES THE PHOTO AND SMILES
SADLY AS HE LOOKS AT IT. THERE'S
AN AWKWARD MOMENT AS ADAM AND JENNY
WAIT FOR PETE TO MAKE THE NEXT
MOVE, BUT PETE CAN'T.

JENNY:

(FEIGNING BRIGHTNESS; TO PETE AND

ADAM) I would ask you to stay.

But there again, no.

PETE:

Can I have a moment with my son?

JENNY:

Sure. (HOLDS HANDS OUT FOR BABY)

When you collect him on Saturday.

RELUCTANTLY, PETE KISSES BABY ADAM
THEN HANDS HIM OVER TO JENNY. WITH
A LOOK AT ADAM, HE LEAVES THE ROOM.
HE PICKS UP HIS BAGS IN THE HALL
AND HEADS OUT OF THE HOUSE. ADAM
LOOKS AT JENNY A BEAT. SHE HOLDS
HIS GAZE. HE KNOWS THERE'S NO
POINT SAYING ANYTHING FURTHER, SO
HE THEN TURNS AND FOLLOWS PETE OUT
OF THE HOUSE. JENNY STAYS STANDING
IN THE ROOM. IT'S ONLY WHEN SHE
HEARS THE FRONT DOOR BEING PULLED
SHUT THAT SHE ALLOWS HER EXPRESSION
TO CHANGE. AS SHE HUGS HER CHILD
AND BREAKS DOWN IN TEARS, WE SEE
WHAT A FACADE HER APPARENT
INVULNERABILITY WAS.

CUT TO SCENE 5 INT DAVID & KAREN'S
KITCHEN

Executive producer *Andy Harries*:

'The storyline for the scene in episode five of series two, where Adam discovers he has testicular cancer, came about as the result of long discussions between Christine, Mike and myself. For some time we had been considering giving one of the characters a serious disease or some kind of cancer. Cancer had come out into the open a bit more with John Diamond's book and newspaper column, and John's writings had a profound effect on me. What makes me proud of the achievements of *Cold Feet* is the way it combines serious issues with comedy. If you take an issue like cancer, which is a fantastically dramatic, depressing, life-threatening problem, but at the same time as doing that you are also able to show the lighter side, then that is extraordinary. And this is something which John Diamond does particularly well. I mean, here is a man who is tragically dying but is able to write columns and indeed make television documentaries which show that while he is in appalling pain and suffering, there is a lighter side to it. And part of the way of coping with a serious illness is the lighter side.

'So basically, we made a decision to give one of the characters cancer. We dismissed the girls quite quickly. We felt that breast cancer had received a lot of publicity and that in a sense it was rather too obvious to do that. We alighted on testicular cancer for three reasons. Firstly, because I myself have had a problem – not actually of cancer – but I do have a testicular problem. It was one of those problems that I developed as a kid and it was fantastically embarrassing for me at the time. One of my testicles is dormant. It was one of those things which was extremely difficult to deal with as a kid and it seemed to me that I would never be able to have children of my own. In fact, I do have children so it's proved not to be a problem, but for a long time I was very concerned about it. So I guess buried deep inside of me was all this trauma, and it was something which I thought Jimmy Nesbitt's character, Adam, would do well.

'Secondly, testicular cancer was not as well known as many other forms although I know a couple of people who have had it and the disease has received more publicity lately. We felt that we could help publicize the illness, particularly with regard to the embarrassment. There's now a sign in the bathroom on our office floor reminding people to get checked. Also, it was a cancer that was appropriate because Adam is a Lothario character so you are giving him a problem directly in contrast to his character.

'Thirdly, it became a storyline we could have a bit of fun with. And there are two scenes that I particularly like and which are in direct contrast. There's the one in the taxi – with

Ricky Tomlinson as the taxi driver – where Adam breaks down. I think it is an extraordinary moment in television. Ricky plays it brilliantly, and so does Jimmy. It's just so real. There's that moment where Adam comes out of hospital and the camera swirls around him. Then he gets into the cab and after a while they stop and have the discussion.

'The other scene I love is where Adam wakes up and is being followed down the street by a bouncing testicle. That was Mike's idea. When we were working out the story, Mike saw it as an opportunity for providing humour by giving Adam a nightmare where he is pursued by a giant testicle. I think he'd watched too many episodes of *The Prisoner* because it's very similar to the ball bouncing across Portmeirion beach. But I thought it was an interesting idea and I'm very proud of that entire storyline. And when I speak in public about *Cold Feet*, that's one of the excerpts that I show because it did move people and it certainly moves me still when I watch it today.

'To my mind, comedy drama is what people want. No one goes through life without laughing and you have to reflect that. Yet so many things on TV don't have any laughs in it, which is bizarre.

Publicist Ian Johnson:

'The second series had just started filming and I hadn't seen the scripts of the later episodes. I was having lunch with Christine Langan and we began a very mundane conversation about financial advisers, and I told her that my partner Chris and I had difficulty getting a mortgage on a flat because he had had testicular cancer. Christine grabbed me by the arm and said, "Oh, my God! I had no idea." People do tend to over-react at the mention of testicular cancer even though it's much more common than they realize and is one of the most curable types of cancer. So I said, "Christine, it's fine. It was years ago and he's completely recovered." And she said: "No, Ian, it's in episode five!"

'I didn't know because episode five was still being written. She said: "Speak to Mike Bullen." So I had long chats with Mike about exactly what happened to Chris, my partner, before, during and after his diagnosis. Mike sent me a draft script and I proofread it with particular regard to the timescale – the stage at which you're actually told things by the doctors. Mike had already researched the storyline with Imperial Cancer Research and I thought he had managed to capture the strange sensation of unreality that you feel at moments like that perfectly. There were a couple of points that I helped clarify and I talked it over with Jimmy, too. I thought he gave an incredible performance and I couldn't believe how the scene in the taxi where it all gets too much for Adam was so accurate. I remember the equivalent when, having been amazingly brave to everybody, Chris suddenly broke down, saying, "I can't be brave, I don't want to have this." It's that moment where the balance tips and you become aware of your own mortality. And just as Chris has gone on radio and made jokes about testicular cancer as a kind of defence, so the scene kicks off with a gag, Adam pulling faces while being examined and being vaguely embarrassed about testicles. But then it stops being a gag as Adam becomes scared. I think that is one of the most significant scenes in *Cold Feet* because it tells people about a disease which they are usually too embarrassed to talk about, but it does so in a comic/dramatic way without being a public health announcement.'

James Nesbitt (Adam):

'We filmed the scene with the giant testicle on the streets of Manchester on a wet Sunday morning. I was wearing very unflattering red Y-fronts and I was freezing. People were watching me and I was feeling like a real idiot. What's more, I was being chased by a giant testicle. Yes, it was very real, very true to life! In fact, the testicle was added in post-production so I had to imagine what was chasing me. And that was interesting to do because I was playing against nothing, really. But it was original and that's one of the things I like about *Cold Feet*.'

The Scripts

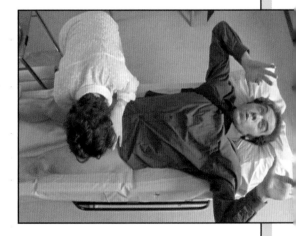

```
SCENE  16 INT
SET  DOCTOR'S CONSULTING ROOM
DAY 3 1600

ADAM:
DOCTOR:

ADAM'S FACE RADIATES SHAME AND
EMBARRASSMENT AS HE LIES ON HIS
BACK ON A CONSULTING TABLE, STARING
UP AT THE CEILING.  (WE CAN'T SEE
THE DOCTOR FIDDLING WITH HIS BALLS).

        ADAM:

It's bruised, isn't it?

AN ATTRACTIVE YOUNG (20S) WOMAN
DOCTOR APPEARS AT THE HEAD OF THE
BED AND STARTS PEELING OFF THE PAIR
OF LATEX GLOVES SHE'S WEARING.

        DOCTOR:

It is.  But that's not primarily

what concerns me.
```

DOCTOR:

Had you felt any discomfort prior

to your sports injury?

ADAM:

Um, no.   No, not really.

THE DOCTOR NODS, AND TURNS AWAY
FROM THE TABLE TO WRITE UP HER
NOTES.

DOCTOR:

You can get dressed now.   (ADAM

DOES)   I'm referring you to the

hospital for an ultrasound.

ADAM:

(TAKEN ABACK)   The hospital?!

DOCTOR:

You have a swelling.

ADAM:

Well, I'm not surprised!   I had a

squash ball straight in the nuts!

DOCTOR:

I think the swelling predates that.

I'm not sure, Adam, but I think you

may have a tumour.

ADAM STARES AT HER IN HORROR, HIS
WORLD COLLAPSING AROUND HIM.

CUT TO SCENE 17 INT ADAM'S LOUNGE
AND **END OF PART ONE**

SCENE 23 EXT
SET HOSPITAL
DAY 4 1740

ADAM:
CABBIE:
Extras:

ADAM, WEARING HIS SUIT, EMERGES FROM
THE ENTRANCE TO A HOSPITAL,
CLUTCHING A LEAFLET SHE'S BEEN
GIVEN. HE LOOKS AT IT. IT'S A COPY
OF THE IMPERIAL CANCER RESEARCH FUND
LEAFLET - "A WHOLE NEW BALL GAME."
SEEING THE COVER, HE WINCES, THEN
LOOKS AWAY, SHAKEN AND
DISORIENTATED. HE STANDS AT THE
SIDE OF THE ROAD, BY THE TAXI STAND,
BUT IS OBLIVIOUS WHEN A BLACK CAB
PULLS UP BESIDE HIM, AND MAKES NO
EFFORT TO GET IN. FINALLY THE
CABBIE WINDS DOWN THE WINDOW ON THE
PASSENGER SIDE AND CALLS TO ADAM.

                CABBIE:

You wanting a taxi, pal?

ADAM IS MOMENTARILY PULLED FROM HIS
REVERIE, SUFFICIENT TO REGISTER THE
CAB. HE CLIMBS IN, AND THE CAB
PULLS AWAY.

CUT TO SCENE 24 INT CAB

SCENE 24 INT
SET CAB
DAY 4 1740

ADAM:
CABBIE:

ADAM'S CAB PULLS AWAY FROM THE
HOSPITAL AND OFF UP THE ROAD.

                CABBIE:

Where to?

                ADAM:

(DISTRACTED) What? Oh, home.

                CABBIE:

Unless you mean my home you're going

to have to give me more of a clue.

                ADAM:

Oh sorry. Clough End. Manyon

Street.

THE CABBIE NODS AND DRIVES ON. A
BEAT.

                CABBIE:

You visiting?

ADAM:

No, I live there.

CABBIE:

I meant the hospital.

ADAM:

Oh. No, I went for a check-up.

CABBIE:

I thought maybe you did. People often look a bit distracted when they come out. Everything okay?

ADAM:

Yeah. Fine. (THE BURDEN OF ADAM'S SECRET PROVES TOO MUCH TO BEAR) No. No, not fine. (BREAKS DOWN IN TEARS) They say I've got cancer.

THE TEARS FLOW, THE FEARS OF THE LAST COUPLE OF DAYS SUDDENLY FLOODING FORTH. THE CABBIE STEALS A CONCERNED GLANCE IN HIS REAR VIEW MIRROR.

CUT TO SCENE 25 INT CAB

SCENE 25 INT
SET CAB
DAY 4 1755

ADAM:
CABBIE:

TRAFFIC THUNDERS PAST AS THE BLACK CAB SITS PARKED AT THE SIDE OF THE ROAD. THE CABBIE IS SITTING IN THE BACK WITH ADAM. ADAM IS NO LONGER CRYING. FOR THE FIRST TIME HE'S ACTUALLY TALKING ABOUT THINGS WITH SOMEONE APART FROM A DOCTOR.

CABBIE:

Can you be sure it's cancer?

ADAM:

Me? I don't have a clue. But I had this ultrasound. I don't know, it like shows the echo or something. Anyway, they reckon there's a 95% chance I've got a malignant tumour.

CABBIE:

So there's a five per cent chance

you haven't?

ADAM:

I think they call that clutching at

straws.

THE CABBIE NODS, ACCEPTING ADAM'S
POINT. THEY'RE SILENT A MOMENT.

ADAM:

Either way, I've got to have a

bollock off.

CABBIE:

Bloody hell. Which one.

ADAM LOOKS AT THE MAN ASKANCE.

ADAM:

Does it matter?

CABBIE:

Does if you want kids. Sons

come from the right bollock. Or so

my nan always said.

ADAM:

Qualified was she?

CABBIE:

Fifteen children.

ADAM'S GESTURE - FAIR ENOUGH. A
BEAT.

AMENDED 28.5.99
ADAM:

They said if I was unhappy about
only having meat and one veg they
could give me a new one. It
wouldn't be real.

CABBIE:

A rubber ball?

ADAM:

Silicon. Like a breast implant.
(BEAT) Except smaller. I said no.
I mean, next time I fly somewhere
I want to be worried about
crashing. Not that my gonads are
gonna explode. (BEAT) That's if I
get to fly anywhere again.
A BEAT.

CABBIE:

You worried about dying?
ADAM NODS.

ADAM:

They reckon if they catch it early
enough the survival rate is 97%,
but there's always that 3%, isn't
there?

CABBIE:

Now who's clutching straws?

ADAM SMILES, ACKNOWLEDGING THE
CABBIE'S POINT.

CUT TO SCENE 26 INT CAB

SCENE 26 INT
SET CAB
DAY 4 1830

ADAM:
CABBIE:
PETE:

ADAM SITS AT THE BACK OF THE CAB AS
IT PULLS UP OUTSIDE HIS HOUSE. HE
GETS OUT, LEAVING THE DOOR OPEN, AS
HE TAKES HIS WALLET OUT. HE LOOKS
THROUGH THE DRIVER'S SIDE WINDOW AT
THE METER - THIS READS £44.20.

   ADAM:

God, we must have been talking a

while. Call it £50, shall we?

HE OFFERS THE CABBIE A HANDFUL OF
BANK NOTES.

   CABBIE:

Put your money away. It's on me.

   ADAM:

But your time. You could have been

working.

THE CABBIE SHRUGS. ADAM OFFERS HIM
A FIVER.

ADAM:

At least let me buy you a drink.

CABBIE:

(TAKING THE NOTE) Okay. I'll drink

to your health. (BEAT) You

still determined not to tell your

friends?

ADAM:

(NODS) I don't think I could cope

with all their sympathy.

THE CABBIE NODS IN UNDERSTANDING,
THEN OFFERS ADAM HIS HAND.

CABBIE:

Well, all the best, Adam.

ADAM:

Thanks, Phil.

THEY SHAKE HANDS, THEN ADAM TURNS TO
ENTER HIS HOUSE, JUST AS PETE COMES
FLYING OUT OF IT.

PETE:

Is that cab free?! I'll have it!

PETE RUSHES PAST ADAM AND JUMPS INTO
THE BACK OF THE CAB.

PETE:

(TO CABBIE) Harper Mews.

ADAM:

(TO PETE) What's happened?

PETE:

Jenny just rang. She wants a

divorce.

ADAM STARES AT PETE IN SHOCK, THEN
LEAPS INTO THE BACK OF THE CAB. THE
CAB PULLS OFF.

PETE:

(TO CABBIE) Oi! Put your meter on!

(TO ADAM, NOT DROPPING HIS VOICE)

You have to watch these cabbies. A

bunch of crooks!

ADAM WINCES AND GLANCES IN THE
CABBIE'S REAR VIEW MIRROR. HE
CATCHES THE CABBIE LOOKING IN THE
MIRROR; THE CABBIE GRINS AT HIM.

CUT TO SCENE 27 INT DAVID & KAREN'S
LOUNGE

SCENE 32 INT
SET OPERATING THEATRE
DAY 5 WEEKDAY 1450

ADAM:
SURGEON:
Anesthetist:
Nurses:
Medical Staff:

ADAM LIES ON THE OPERATING TABLE
WITH A GAGGLE OF MEDICAL STAFF
AROUND HIM - SURGEON, ANESTETIST
AND NURSES. THE ANESTETIST
REMOVES A MASK FROM ADAM'S FACE.
AS THE SURGEON SPEAKS, ADAM BEGINS
TO FEEL WOOZY AND FINDS IT
DIFFICULT TO FOCUS ON THE SURGEON'S
FACE AND MAKE OUT DISTINCTLY WHAT
HE'S SAYING.

SURGEON:

Right, I'll be making an incision

of about four inches in length,

in your groin and then removing the

testicle and spermatic cords.

SURGEON: CONTD

You'll be under general

anesthetic, which should start

to kick in any time now.

AS THE SURGEON REACHES THIS POINT
IN HIS DISCOURSE, ADAM LOSES
CONSCIOUSNESS COMPLETELY, THE FACES
IN THE OPERATING THEATRE LEAKING
AWAY LIKE ONE OF THOSE SCREENSAVERS
THAT BLEED FROM THE TOP OF THE
SCREEN TO THE BOTTOM. REVEALED
BEHIND THIS IMAGE IS THE NEXT
SCENE...

CUT TO SCENE 33 EXT CENTRAL
MANCHESTER

SCENE 33 EXT
SET CENTRAL MANCHESTER
DAY (FANTASY) 1515

RACHEL:
ADAM:
Shoppers:

RACHEL IS STANDING ALONE, WEEKEND
SHOPPERS DRIFTING PAST, WHEN ADAM
SUDDENLY RACES UP IN A PAIR OF
UNDERPANTS (Y-FRONT TYPE *NOT*
BOXERS!). HE'S EXTREMELY AGITATED,
LOOKING AROUND HIM AS THOUGH
EXPECTING TO BE ATTACKED OR
ARRESTED OR SOMETHING.

ADAM:

Rachel! Rachel!

RACHEL:

Adam!

ADAM:

(LOOKING AROUND) Look, I don't

have much time, so just hear me

out...

RACHEL:

(INTERRUPTING) You're wearing underpants.

ADAM:

Yes, I know. Now, listen...

RACHEL:

(INTERRUPTING) Why are you wearing underpants?

ADAM:

Because if I wasn't I'd be naked.

(BEAT) Do they look lop-sided?

RACHEL TILTS HER HEAD TO ASSESS THE SITUATION.

RACHEL:

Are you dressing to the left?

ADAM:

(CHECKING AROUND HIM) It doesn't matter. Listen, this is important. I shouldn't have left it this late to tell you. You are the love of my life. I'll never love another woman like I've loved you. Like I *love* you!

ADAM IS ABOUT TO SAY MORE WHEN RACHEL, SEEING SOMETHING APPROACHING, LEAPS BACK.

RACHEL:

Adam! Look out!

ADAM TURNS ROUND, JUST IN TIME TO SEE A GIANT TESTICLE, STRANDS OF HAIR HANGING FROM IT, BEARING DOWN ON HIM. HIS FACE REGISTERS HORROR. THE SPEED OF THE TESTICLE MEANS HE NEVER HAS THE CHANCE TO MOVE. HE MERELY THROWS UP HIS HANDS IN A FUTILE ATTEMPT TO SAVE HIMSELF AS, LIKE AN AVALANCHE, THE GIANT TESTICLE BOWLS HIM OVER, RUNNING HIM DOWN.

CUT TO SCENE 34 INT HOSPITAL WARD

SCENE 34 INT
SET HOSPITAL WARD
DAY 5 1735

ADAM:
SURGEON:
RACHEL:
PETE:
JENNY:
DAVID:
KAREN:
JOSH:
BABY ADAM:
Six foot Rabbit:
Nurse:
Medical Staff:
Other Patients & visitors:

ADAM SITS BOLT UPRIGHT IN BED,
SWEATING. HE SEES THE SURGEON
SITTING BESIDE THE BED.

SURGEON:

Ah! You've come round. Well, that

seemed to go off very well.

ADAM:

It was a success?

SURGEON:

Too early to say, I'm afraid.

Until we have the results back from

the lab.

ADAM BECOMES AWARE THAT THERE'S
SOMEONE ELSE STANDING ON THE OTHER
SIDE OF THE BED. HE TURNS HIS HEAD
TO LOOK, AND SEES A SIX-FOOT TALL
RABBIT, WEARING A WHITE COAT AND A
STETHOSCOPE ROUND HIS NECK. ADAM
TURNS BACK TO THE SURGEON.

ADAM:

Should he be here?

SURGEON:

Not unless he's done six years

medical training, no.

ADAM:

I'm still hallucinating, right?

SURGEON:

For your sake, I certainly hope so.

ADAM LETS HIMSELF FALL BACK ONTO
THE BED AND CLENCHES HIS EYES SHUT.
IT'S WHILE HE'S LYING LIKE THIS
THAT HE HEARS RACHEL'S VOICE NEARBY.

RACHEL: OOV

Thanks. I'll just sit here in case

he wakes up.

ADAM OPENS ONE EYE AND SEES A NURSE
NODDING TO RACHEL BEFORE WALKING
AWAY. RACHEL DOESN'T LOOK AT ADAM,
EXPECTING HIM TO STILL BE ASLEEP.
INSTEAD SHE ARRANGES HERSELF FOR A
LONG STAY.

   ADAM:

You weren't crushed by the giant

testicle then?

   RACHEL:

(JUMPS) Oooh! You made me jump!

   ADAM:

I'm hallucinating, you know.

   RACHEL:

Well, that'll be the anestetic.

What can you see?

A BEAT. IT STRIKES ADAM AS ODD
THAT THE SUBJECT OF THIS
HALLUCINATION IS TALKING TO HIM.

   ADAM:

You.

   RACHEL:

Really. And what am I doing?

   ADAM:

Sitting by the side of the hospital

bed talking to me.

NOW IT'S RACHEL'S TURN TO BE THROWN.

   RACHEL:

How do you know it's a

hallucination and not real life?

   ADAM:

You mean, like what's the sound of

one hand clapping?

RACHEL LOOKS CONFUSED - SHE'S NOT
SURE IF THAT'S WHAT SHE MEANS OR
NOT.

   ADAM:

Because the only people I've told

are Pete and Jenny and I told them

not to tell anyone. Quid pro quo

(SIC), in the real world you don't

know.

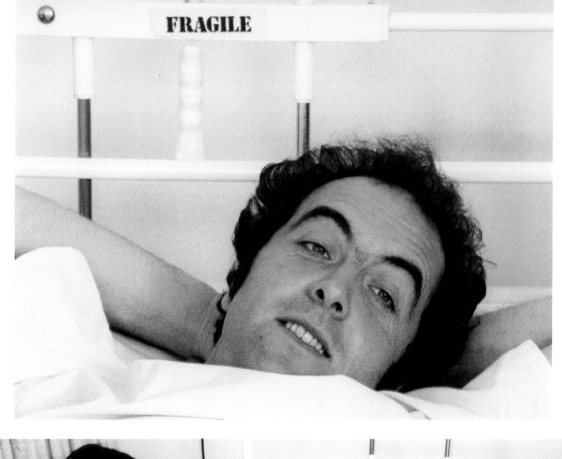

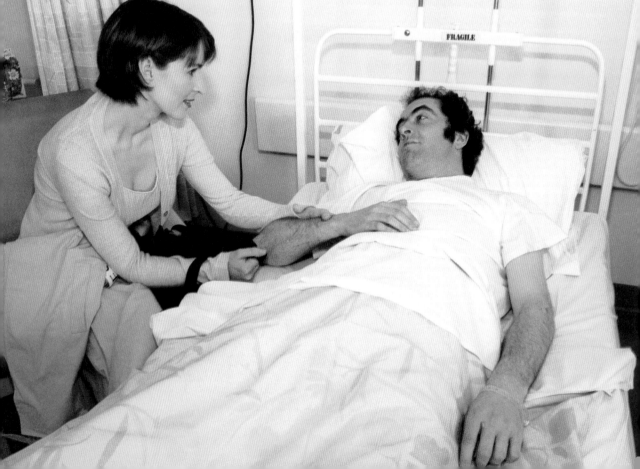

RACHEL:

Unless they felt that with something as important as this, they owed it to you to break their promise and tell the people closest to you.

ADAM WEIGHS UP THE LIKELIHOOD OF THIS.

ADAM:

Maybe. But if that were the case what's that giant rabbit doing over there?

ADAM POINTS ACROSS THE WARD TO WHERE THE GIANT RABBIT FROM HIS EARLIER HALLUCINATION IS STANDING BY THE SIDE OF SOMEONE'S BED.

RACHEL:

Collecting for the medical school's rag week.

AND SURE ENOUGH, THE RABBIT PULLS OUT A BUCKET WHICH JANGLES BEING FULL OF CASH, AND SOMEONE VISITING A PATIENT THROWS SOME COINS IN. A BEAT; ADAM LOOKS UNEASY.

ADAM:

They told you?

RACHEL LOOKS APOLOGETIC. ADAM GRIMACES.

ADAM:

You're the last person I wanted to know. Well, apart from David and Karen.

DAVID: OOV

There he is!

ADAM'S HEAD TURNS TOWARDS THE VOICE HE'S JUST HEARD. CROSSING THE WARD TOWARDS HIM ARE PETE, JENNY, DAVID AND KAREN, CARRYING THEIR JRESPECTIVE CHILDREN AND BEARING GIFTS - FLOWERS, FRUIT, BOOKS, CHOCOLATES, MAGAZINES, EVEN A LARGE JIGSAW PUZZLE. THEY ALL WAVE WITH BRAVURA SMILES. ADAM LOOKS AT RACHE; SHE SHRUGS - "SORRY".

CUT TO END OF PART TWO AND SCENE 35 INT HOSPITAL WARD

SCENE 35 INT
SET HOSPITAL WARD
DAY 5 1740

ADAM:
RACHEL:
DAVID:
KAREN:
PETE:
JENNY:
JOSH:
BABY ADAM:

RACHEL, DAVID, KAREN, PETE AND
JENNY HUDDLE ROUND ADAM'S BED.
JENNY HOLDS BABY ADAM; JOSH CLIMBS
ON ADAM'S BED. KAREN ARRANGES HIS
FLOWERS.

PETE:

(HANDING ADAM A BOOK) I brought

you that book you had your eyes on

the other day.

ADAM:

Oh, right.

JENNY:

We found it when Pete was unpacking

his stuff.

AMENDED 28.5.99
**ADAM LOOKS FROM JENNY TO PETE -
JENNY AND PETE BOTH LOOK
EMBARRASSED.**

JENNY:

We're making an effort.

PETE:

Yeah, yeah, to give it a go.

JENNY:

Yeah.

ADAM:

(INTRIGUED) Really? That's good.

(ACCEPTING THAT HE SHOULDN'T GO

THERE) Okay...

JOSH:

(TO DAVID) I want a chocolate!

DAVID:

Well, you'll have to ask uncle Adam.

JOSH:

(TO ADAM) I want a chocolate!

ADAM:

Sure.

IN HIS EXCITEMENT, JOSH BOUNCES ON
THE BED, DANGEROUSLY CLOSE TO
ADAM'S GROIN.

ADAM:

(TO DAVID) Can you just make sure

he doesn't...

ADAM POINTS IN THE GENERAL
DIRECTION OF HIS GROIN.

DAVID:

Sorry. Josh! Off the bed.

JOSH:

(PROTESTING) Ohhhhhhhhhh!

KAREN:

(TO JOSH, STERNLY) Off!

JOSH RELUCTANTLY CLIMBS DOWN.
JENNY OPENS THE BOX OF CHOCOLATES
AND JOSH CHOOSES ONE. JENNY OFFERS
THE BOX TO ADAM WHO, STILL FEELING
A BIT GROGGY, DECLINES. JEN THEN
TAKES A CHOCOLATE HERSELF AND
OFFERS THEM ROUND - EVERYONE ELSE
TAKES ONE.

RACHEL:

(TO ADAM, LIGHTLY) So... how are

you feeling?

ADAM:

Well, I'm not feeling myself.

Until the scars have healed it

wouldn't be advisable.

NO ONE'S QUITE SURE HOW TO REACT TO
THIS COMMENT. THEY LOOK A BIT
AWKWARD, WHICH OF COURSE IS THE
LAST THING ADAM WANTS.

ADAM:

Guys, come on. WE all know what I

came in here with. And what I'll

be leaving without.

JENNY:

You know... you mustn't be

embarrassed.

ADAM:

Because I'm half the man I used to

be?

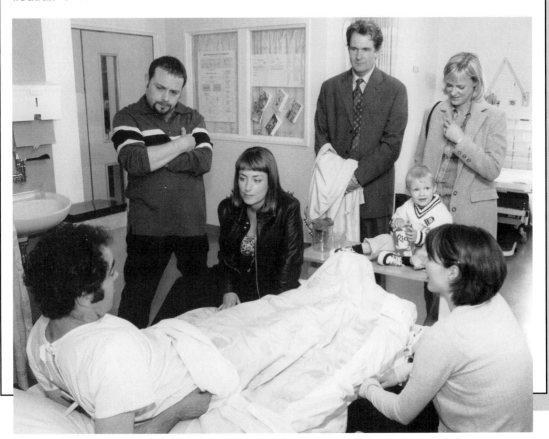

GENERAL MURMURS OF PROTEST FROM
ADAM'S FRIENDS.

KAREN:

You mustn't see it like that.

RACHEL:

No. It doesn't make any

difference. (BEAT; UNCERTAINLY)

Does it?

ADAM:

Will if I need chemotherapy.

PETE:

You know, I bet there've been loads

of famous people who only had one.

ADAM:

You mean apart from Hitler?

PETE:

(A RELUCTANT ADMISSION) Well,

yeah, Hitler is the most famous.

And to be honest, I'm not even sure

he did. I think they were just

trying to ridicule him.

ADAM:

(SARCASTICALLY) Great.

RACHEL:

Bruce Lee only had one.

ADAM:

(GENUINELY INTERESTED) Really?

RACHEL:

(LOOKS DOUBTFUL) Oh, I might have

just made that up.

ADAM ROLLS HIS EYES IN EXASPERATION.

JENNY:

Well, either way, he lived a full

and active life.

ADAM:

Till his death at the age of 32.

PETE:

Yeah, but that wasn't cancer.

AGAIN, PETE'S CONTRIBUTION IS NOT
AS SUCCESSFUL AS HE MIGHT HAVE
HOPED. A BEAT.

ADAM:

Look guys, I really appreciate you

coming. But I'd like you to go now.

JENNY:

Shall we come tomorrow?

ADAM GIVES HER A FIXED LOOK - "WHAT
DO YOU THINK?"

JENNY:

Maybe the day after.

CUT TO SCENE 36 EXT THE HOSPITAL

Director Pete Travis:

'When I started episode six of series two, we didn't have a location. But the production manager had a Roman Polanski film set on Holy Island (Lindisfarne) and when he showed it to us, Mike Bullen and I were so inspired by the beauty and dramatic possibilities of the island that we went straight up there the next day. After that, Mike wrote the script in something like two days.

'The episode is Mike's version of *The Big Chill*. David has decided to take all of his friends away for the Millennium to this remote castle and we see how they cope with the various dramas in their relationships and with each other in a different environment. It ties up Adam and Rachel's romance, Pete and Jenny's awkward situation, and Karen learning that she is pregnant. We shot the interior of the castle at Hoghton Tower, near Preston, but the exteriors were done over five days on Lindisfarne.'

Helen Baxendale (Rachel):

'My favourite *Cold Feet* location was definitely Lindisfarne and my favourite scene was Fay and I walking along the beach, just chatting about love. It was a beautiful day in this stunning place with a huge beach and an enormous horizon. It was also a nice change because I hardly ever get to do scenes with Fay. And I liked Fay's hat!'

Hermione Norris (Karen):

'It was my first visit to Lindisfarne and I just found it an amazing place with a magical atmosphere. It was spectacular, stunning and very special, and I would love to go back there.'

Fay Ripley (Jenny):

'At one point on Holy Island I had to come in with my screen son in my arms and say something like: "I'm going to give him his bath." As we did the take, he threw up all over me – very chunky sick, a whole risotto. We had very little time and I was literally stinking of baby's sick. I felt so sorry for him and I think we got the other baby in because we used twins, but whenever I look at that scene today, I can still see the stains.

'For every scene I do with a child, my pockets are stuffed full of melted chocolate buttons and all sorts of bribery. As the kids get older, it's just hard cash. I say: "One more take, and it's 50p this time." But these days with some kids, unless you've got a tenner in your pocket, it's not going to get shot.'

SCENE 34 EXT
SET OUTSIDE THE CASTLE
DAY 2 1200

RACHEL:
JENNY:

RACHEL AND JENNY ARE WALKING
TOGETHER OUTSIDE THE CASTLE.

          JENNY:

You and Adam are getting on well.

          RACHEL:

What makes you say that?

          JENNY:

Seeing you together.

(MEANINGFULLY) Hearing you

together.

RACHEL DOESN'T GET THE REFERENCE.

          RACHEL:

Yeah, I think we've finally put

Kris and all that behind us.

          JENNY:

(SQUEEZING RACHEL'S ARM) I'm glad.

RACHEL SMILES.

Cold Feet

RACHEL:

You and Pete seem to be doing all right too.

JENNY:

Yeah. We do, don't we? You know, I always though if a relationship went sour, then that was it. Forget it. You can't fall in love (with the same person) again. But maybe you can.

RACHEL:

(OPTIMISTICALLY) Yeah! like lightening striking in the same place twice.

JENNY:

(CONFUSED) They say it doesn't.

RACHEL:

Oh. (BEAT) Bad example.

JENNY:

(REFERRING TO HER AND PETE) Well, anyway, so far so good.

RACHEL SMILES REASSURINGLY. A BEAT.

JENNY:

God, I love it here. It's so restful.

CUT TO SCENE 35 EXT OUTSIDE THE CASTLE

Jacey Salles (Ramona):

'I love the scene where Ramona screams at her boyfriend Javier in Spanish above English sub-titles. The whole group are at the castle and Rachel asks Ramona why she is with them and not her boyfriend. Ramona says, "We've sort of discussed it" and there's a flashback to where she and Javier have just had sex and he announces he's going back to Spain. Then Ramona starts screaming in Spanish. I had to brush up on my Spanish for that scene. I'm half-Spanish – my Dad is Spanish and I spent eight years in Ibiza – and I used to be pretty fluent. They write it all in English and leave it to me to put it in Spanish because when they do script it, the grammar's all wrong. We had to do the row scene quite a few times, which meant that I was very hoarse by the end. I had to throw a shoe at Javier Llamas (who plays my boyfriend) but instead of narrowly missing him, as it was supposed to do, it whacked him in the face. Luckily, he was OK, but I do hurl a mean shoe. On another take, the lamp fell over by itself, the door slammed and opened again, and I just collapsed in a dramatic heap and went "Ugh!" in despair. Funnily enough, that was the shot they used in the end.'

The Scripts

```
SCENE  39 INT
SET  RAMONA'S BEDROOM
NIGHT (FLASHBACK) 2000

RAMONA:
JAVIER:

WE JOIN RAMONA AND HER SEXY SPANISH
BARECHESTED BOYFRIEND JAVIER IN MID
BLAZING ROW.  THEY SHOUT AT EACH
OTHER IN SPANISH, GESTICULATING
WILDLY; THE WORDS FLOWING OUT IN A
BABBLE.  AS THEY NEAR THE END OF
EACH SPEECH THE WORDS ARE TRANSLATED
IN AN ENGLISH SUBTITLE.
```

```
          RAMONA:

(SHOUTS IN SPANISH)  Why do you

suddenly tell me this now?  I am

your girlfriend!  You should want to

spend New Year with me.  Not go back

to Spain!  Why do you want to go

back to Spain?

(ENGLIGH SUB-TITLE)  Why do you want

to go home?
```

Why do you want to go home?

JAVIER:

(SHOUTS IN SPANISH) For some peace
and quiet. So I don't have to put
up with this sort of hysteria.
You're crazy, you know that? Why
shouldn't I do what I want? Go home
if I want to. See in the New Year
with my friends. (ENGLISH
SUB-TITLE) To see my friends.

A BEAT. RAMONA'S EYES NARROW.

RAMONA:

(IN SPANISH; SUSPICIOUSLY)
Isabella? (ENGLISH SUB-TITLE)
Isabella?

Isabella?

JAVIER:

(SHOUTS IN SPANISH) Isabella!
Always Isabella! She hasn't been my
girlfriend for more than a year now
but you're convinced I'm still going
out with her! I don't even know if
she'll be there. And I couldn't
care less either way! (ENGLISH
SUB-TITLE) No.

RAMONA'S EYES WIDEN IN ANGER AT WHAT
SHE SEES AS AN OBVIOUS LIE, THEN SHE
STARTS HURLING ANYTHING SHE CAN GET
HER HANDS ON AT JAVIER - BOOKS, A
HAIRBRUSH, MAKE-UP, SHOES ETC.

No

RAMONA:

(SCREAMS IN SPANISH) I hate you! I
hope I never see you again. I hope
your plane crashes and you drown.
Or get eaten by sharks. Whichever
is more painful. (SUBSIDES IN SOBS)
ENGLISH SUB-TITLE Have a nice time.

CUT BACK TO SCENE 40 EXT CASTLE

Director Pete Travis:

'The key moment in this episode is where Adam and Pete get stranded in a boat out at sea in the middle of the night. That took two days to film. We were shooting in the middle of June and in that part of the country there are only about three hours of night at that time of the year. The other problem was the tide. We had tide charts – in fact, co-producer David Meddick became something of a tide expert – but it can still surprise you how quickly it comes in and out. One minute, you could be up to your chest in water; two hours later, there is barely enough to cover your feet. Directors want to be able to control everything, but you can't make the tide stay in and you can't make the sun go back down again. So it was a constant race against time.

'Although the weather was kind to us, it wasn't an easy shoot and was pretty uncomfortable for the crew, dressed in waders up to their midriff. It made things like going to the toilet difficult and also we had to wade through 250 yards of water every time we wanted to change a magazine on the camera. But happily, that adversity seemed to bring out the best in everyone.

'Jimmy and John did all the scenes in the boat except when the fireworks from the castle set it on fire. Then we had stuntmen jumping out of the burning boat. And although on screen it looks as if fireworks landed really close to the actors, in fact they were at least 50 yards away. But we shot it on a long lens to make it appear closer. I was pleased with the firework display. We had a consignment of fireworks, but the first two takes we did just didn't seem big enough. They didn't look as spectacular as I wanted. So the special effects guys told me I could go for broke by throwing everything in. So we went for the big one and it worked.'

John Thomson (Pete):

'I got a black eye on Holy Island (Lindisfarne) as a result of an encounter with an anchor. I had to pull the anchor up, but the chain on the anchor was heavier than the anchor itself. I pulled in the rope attached to the chain with no problem, but as I was yanking on the chain, the anchor flew up and hit me in the eye. They had to hide the bruise with make-up. I was very lucky – it could have been a lot worse. The nurse on Lindisfarne turned out to be the owner of the sweet shop and the ice cream place. It

SCENE 53 EXT
SET SEA
NIGHT 2 2130

ADAM:
PETE:

THE ARGUMENT HAS BLOWN OVER. ADAM
AND PETE ARE NOW SITTING IN THE
BOAT, CALMLY AWAITING THEIR FATE.
THEY BOB IN SILENCE A MOMENT.

        PETE:

Adam? You remember that time you

got suspended from school?

        ADAM:

(SMILES AT THE MEMORY) For putting

potassium permanganate in the

swimming pool.

A BEAT.

        PETE:

It was me that grassed you.

ADAM LOOKS PETE; HE NEVER KNEW
THIS.

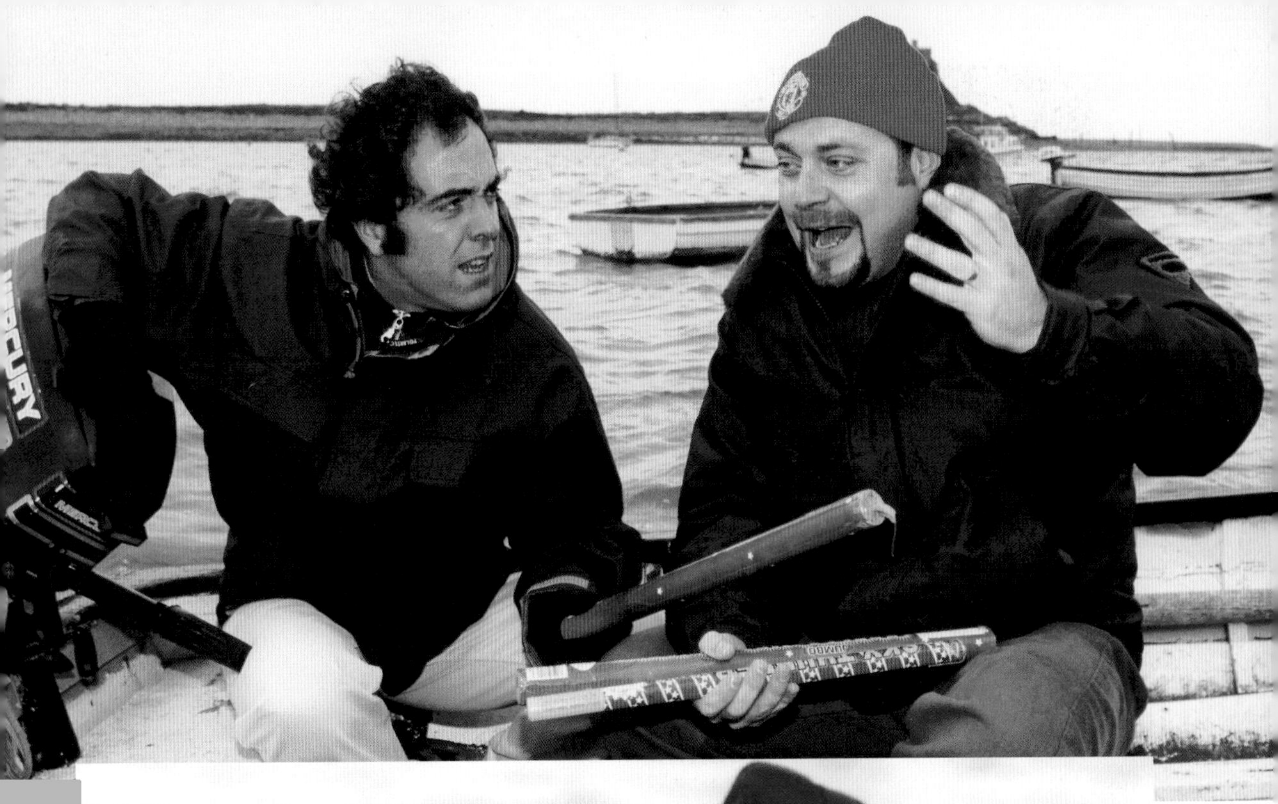

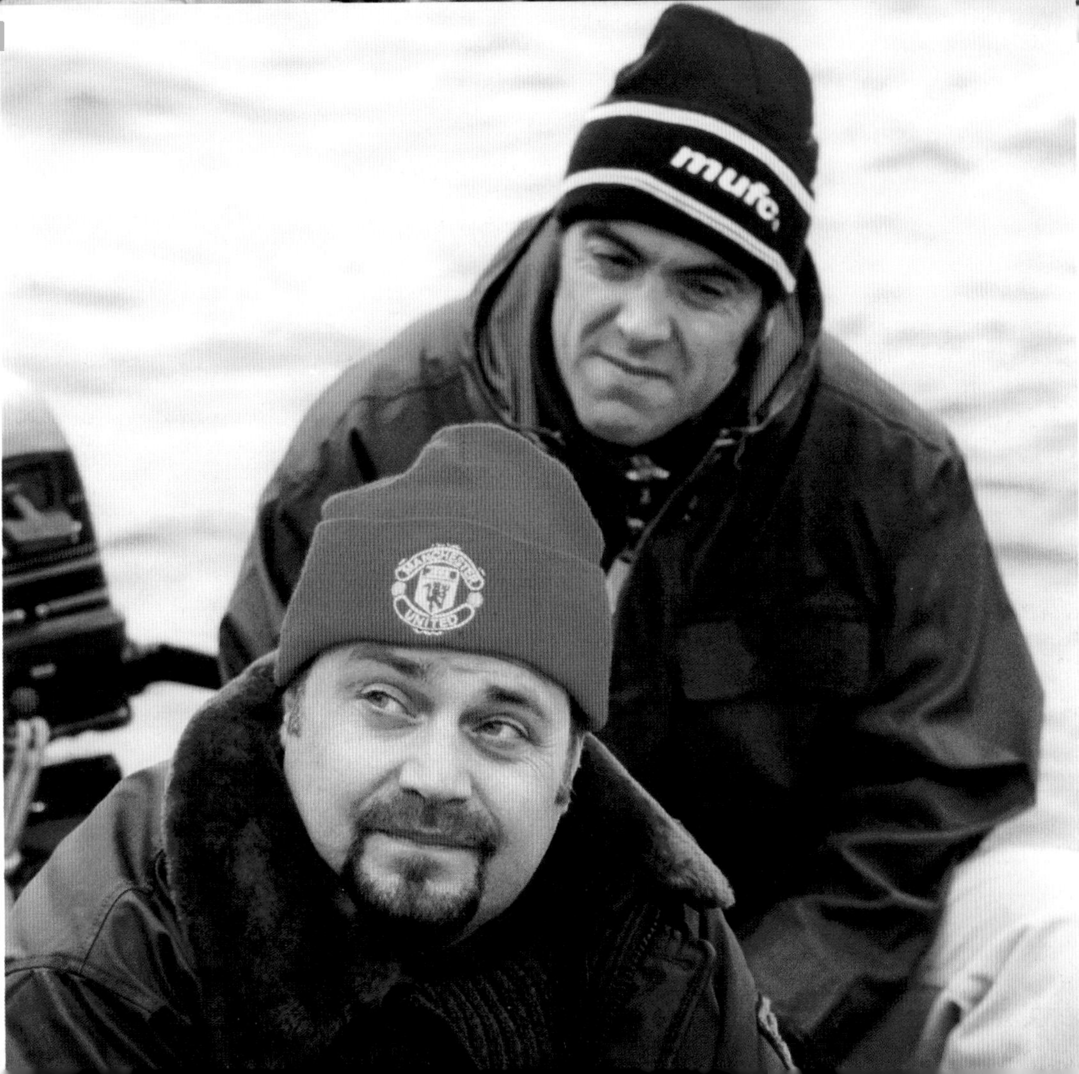
mufc.

PETE:

(SHRUGS APOLOGETICALLY) I was

pissed off cos you wouldn't give me

Joe Jordan. He was all I needed to

finish the set. Anyway... I'm

sorry.

ADAM NODS - "THAT'S OKAY". A BEAT.

ADAM:

I'm dying for a piss.

HE RISES AND TURNS TO PEE OFF THE
SIDE OF THE BOAT, AND IT'S AT THAT
MOMENT THAT HE SEES THE CASTLE ALL
LIT UP ABOVE THEM, AND THE
HEADLIGHTS OF THE TWO CARS SHINING
OUT IN DIFFERENT DIRECTIONS.

ADAM:

Pete! Look!

PETE FOLLOWS ADAM'S GAZE.

PETE:

Oh, thank God!!

THEY START WAVING AND SHOUTING THEN
REALISE THAT THIS IS DOING THEM NO
GOOD.

ADAM:

They won't be able to hear. You

got a lighter on you?

PETE:

They won't be able to see that!

ADAM:

No, you bollix! We'll light this

rag and wave it.

PETE:

Brilliant!

HE FISHES IN HIS POCKET FOR HIS
LIGHTER AS ADAM PICKS UP THE RAG.
THEY ATTEMPT TO LIGHT IT.

CUT TO SCENE 54 EXT CASTLE

SCENE 54 EXT
SET CASTLE
NIGHT 2 2130

DAVID:
KAREN:
RACHEL:
JENNY:

DAVID, KAREN, RACHEL AND JENNY ARE
STILL HUNTING AROUND CALLING PETE
AND ADAM'S NAME, WHEN RACHEL
NOTICES A SMALL LIGHT AWAY IN THE
DISTANCE.

RACHEL:

Look! What's that?

DAVID, KAREN AND JENNY JOIN HER AND
PEER OUT AT THE DISTANT FLAME WHICH
WAVES FROM SIDE TO SIDE.

CUT TO SCENE 55 EXT SEA

SCENE 55 EXT
SET SEA
NIGHT 2 2130

ADAM:
PETE:

ADAM IS WAVING THE RAG AROUND ABOVE
HIS HEAD. THE RAG BURNS DOWN,
UNTIL IT BECOMES UNCOMFORTABLE, AND
ADAM STARTS HOPPING ABOUT WITH THE
PAIN.

PETE:

Throw it overboard! Throw it

overboard!

ADAM ATTEMPTS TO HURL THE BURNING
RAG AWAY, BUT BEING NERVOUS OF
GETTING BURNT DOESN'T MAKE A GOOD
JOB OF IT. NOR DOES THE WIND HE'S
THROWING INTO HELP. BOTH CONSPIRE
TO BLOW THE RAG BACK INTO THE
DINGHY, WHERE IT QUICKLY SETS LIGHT
TO THE PIZZA BOXES.

PETE:

Ah! We're on fire!!!

ADAM:

Abandon ship! Abandon ship!

PETE:

Abandon ship! Abandon ship!

PETE AND ADAM HURL THEMSELVES OUT
OF THE BOAT, EXPECTING TO BE
SUBMERGED BY THE SURROUNDING WATER.
TO THEIR CONSTERNATION, THEY LAND
IN THE COUPLE OF INCHES OF WATER
THAT'S COVERING THE CAUSEWAY NOW
THAT THE TIDE IS AGAIN GOING OUT.
IT TAKES ADAM AND PETE A MOMENT TO
REALISE WHAT'S HAPPENING.   THEN
THEY HAUL THEMSELVES TO THEIR FEET.

ADAM:

The tide's gone out! We're on the

causeway!

PETE:

We're saved!!

DELERIOUS WITH DELIGHT, THEY HUG
EACH OTHER AND DANCE AROUND,THE
BOAT STILL BURNING BEHIND THEM.
THEN AT THE SAME MOMENT, THE BREAK
OUT OF THEIR EMBRACE AND STARE AT
ONE ANOTHER IN HORROR.

                PETE/ADAM
(IN UNISON) The fireworks!!

THEY BREAK AWAY FROM EACH OTHER AND
TAKE OFF UP THE CAUSEWAY, RUNNING
TOWARDS THE CASTLE, JUST AS THE
FIREWORKS START TO EXPLODE BEHIND
THEM.

CUT TO SCENE 56 EXT CASTLE

SCENE 56 EXT
SET   THE CASTLE
NIGHT 2 2130

RACHEL:
JENNY:
DAVID:
KAREN:
PETE:
ADAM:

RACHEL, JENNY, DAVID AND KAREN ARE
STANDING LOOKING OUT AT THE SEA AS
A MAGNIFICENT FIREWORK DISPLAY
SUDDENLY EXPLODES INTO THE SKY AND
ILLUMINATES THE SURROUNDING AREA.
TWO HUDDLED FIGURES CAN BE SEEN
RUNNING FRANTICALLY ACROSS THE
CAUSEWAY AWAY FROM THE SCENE.
RACHEL AND JENNY AND DAVID AND
KAREN EXCHANGE ASTONISHED LOOKS.

CUT TO **END OF PART TWO** AND SCENE 57

Cold Feet – the best bits...

was a bit like the film *The Wicker Man* without the occult sub-text.

'I didn't know we had bog-standard fireworks. When they went off on the boat, I literally went, "My God, is that it?" But unbeknown to me, they did more. The thing is, the area is a nature reserve, so you've got to be careful. We filmed the boat scene from five in the afternoon till five in the morning. The hours weren't too bad. We had to wade out to the boat, but the tide was so fast that they had to keep moving the boat back.

'Also on Lindisfarne, Jimmy and I improvised a ventriloquist and his dummy routine, where the boys do a turn for the girls. That was a laugh. Being the dummy came naturally. It was a bit near the bone with all the "geaver" stuff, but we got away with it.

'I do the job of two people on *Cold Feet* because I try and keep everyone's spirits up by clowning. I love my false teeth – they're a winner. And wigs, too. Put me in any wig and it fits. I don't know what it is, I've just got a face that takes a wig. I get up to all sorts. When Hermione was being made up with her eyes shut, I took the brush off the make-up artist and started peppering Hermione's face with the brush quite forcibly. She wondered what the hell was going on, opened her eyes and saw it was me doing it!'

Publicist Ian Johnson:

'As all six of the cast were together, I decided that Lindisfarne presented us with the last opportunity to shoot a *TV Times* cover. So we all turned up on this small island, where we had to get on and off at particular times of day because of the tide – two stylists, a photographer, an assistant, bags and bags of designer clothes and mountains of equipment. The unit base was the wooden village hall where we'd been assured that we had stacks of space to shoot the cover. We did it the day after John nearly brained himself with the anchor. Because he's always going around wearing false teeth and playing practical jokes on people, at first everyone thought his black eye was a joke, too. People were laughing at him, thinking that he'd got make-up to put a black eye on him. Then they realized that it was real and that he had almost blinded himself. So John had a black eye and a splitting headache, and everyone had turned up at this tiny place ready to shoot all through the night and I, in my wisdom, had decided to shoot the cover of *TV Times*. The village hall was so tiny that the cast got changed in an area, this Fifties-style kitchen, where the WI normally made their cream teas. To make matters worse, as we set up the shoot, I

Cold Feet – the best bits...

hadn't noticed that the hall wasn't even free at that time – it was being used as the crew canteen because there was no catering bus. So the cast stepped out to find themselves doing the shoot in front of 30 members of the crew, eating chips and beans. Luckily, the cover looked fantastic and the village hall's wooden backdrop with its little stage fooled everyone. People kept asking me: "Where did you find that New York loft apartment?" '

Scenes to Come – Series Three:

The third series of *Cold Feet* is set six months on from the end of the second. Adam Williams and Rachel Louise Bradley are still an item. They had split up when she hit him with the double whammy of an ex-husband (Kris with a 'K') and a pregnancy. After having a secret abortion, she was reunited with Adam in the wake of his cancer diagnosis. Their relationship seems stronger, more stable, than ever. He is a systems analyst and impulsive romantic; she is in advertising.

'Rachel is learning about things,' says Helen Baxendale, 'becoming more mature. She loves Adam. Before she was confused about her feelings, but now she knows.'

David Marsden, a management consultant with City firm BZQ, remains married to publishing editor Karen, who is expecting their second child. He has got over the shock of being made redundant and she has got over her mid-life crisis. They have a volatile Spanish nanny, Ramona, who looks after their son, Josh.

'Karen lost her identity with her first baby,' says Hermione Norris, 'came into her own and developed, but now she's back to domesticity with another baby on the way. This means she has to take maternity leave from work.'

Pete and Jenny Gifford have split up by the start of series three in the wake of Pete's affair at the office with Amy, which in itself was something of a knee-jerk reaction to Jenny's confession that she loved Adam. Pete and Adam are mates again. Pete – a child in a man's body – works as a drone in an insurance agency, processing the claims. Although he and Adam both sit at desks, Adam has an interesting job whereas Pete is just clockwatching.

Fay Ripley says: 'People ask me: "Are you and Pete going to get back together?" And I say: "I'm afraid I don't know." Which is true – I don't.'

'Pete's not a million miles from me,' admits John Thomson, 'except that he likes football and I can't stand it.'

Cold Feet – the best bits...

New Characters:

Robert, Jenny's new boyfriend, is a dotcom millionaire. He meets her via David and falls for her in a big way. Very rich, charming and marginally younger than Jenny, he fulfils some of her short-term dreams although in the long term, the relationship makes her ask questions about what she really wants from life and how she truly feels about Pete.

Heather is Karen's mother, who has been living the life of an ex-pat on the Costa del Sol. She's not mutton, but she's not lamb either. Her dress sense is slightly too loud and she drinks too much. Ostensibly, she has come to England to help Karen with the second birth but Karen soon discovers that her mother has actually left her father.

Jessica Barnes is an attractive, young political activist for the local residents' association, who is also a campaigner for the Labour Party. She comes into David's life when she knocks on his door seeking support for a campaign to prevent the building of a supermarket on the site of a children's playground. David is smitten with the dynamic Jessica and starts fantasizing about her, not because his own marriage is in trouble but simply because she is so irresistible. She in turn clearly likes him – which he finds enormously flattering – but she is extremely self-possessed and in control.

Brodie is a glamorous, wandering photo journalist who offers an insight into Karen's past. He represents the route she might have taken, had she not met David. Ironically, at a time when her husband is being tempted, Brodie reminds her of exactly why she went for someone like David.

Matthew is Pete's middle-aged, gay flatmate. He is quite an avuncular figure – not at all camp – and is a good friend to Pete in troubled times.

Jane Fitzpatrick is Adam's first true love. He meets her again on a trip to Northern Ireland and the old flame is in danger of being rekindled.